'.45-70' Rifles

'.45-70' RIFLES

Jack Behn

STACKPOLE BOOKS

Copyright © 1956 by Jack Behn

Published by
STACKPOLE BOOKS
5067 Ritter Road
Mechanicsburg, PA 17055
www.stackpolebooks.com

All rights reserved, including the right to reproduce this book or portions thereof in any form or by any means, electronic or mechanical, including photocopying, recording, or by any information storage and retrieval system, without permission in writing from the publisher. All inquiries should be addressed to Stackpole Books, 5067 Ritter Road, Mechanicsburg, PA 17055.

Printed in the United States of America

10 9 8 7 6 5 4 3 2 1

First edition

Cover design by Wendy A. Reynolds

ISBN-13: 978-0-8117-0446-5
ISBN-10: 0-8117-0446-7

Cataloging-in-Publication Data is on file with the Library of Congress

DEDICATION

To my wife

LOUISE

*who has had the patience
to live nine years
with a gun collector*

Preface

This book is the saga of the .45-70, our Government Service cartridge through the most colorful years in the settlement and taming of the West. From the early 70's to the War of 1898 with Spain, a period of some twenty-five years, covered the reduction of our powerful plains Indian tribes. Kiowas, Comanches, Arapahoes, Crows, Cheyennes, Sioux, Blackfeet, Nez Perce, Modoc, Shoshone and Apache tribes all played their part in the fight to stop the white man from destroying their buffalo and other game and taking over their hunting grounds. Many of these tribes were the finest light cavalry upon which the sun ever shone, and gave the U. S. Army many years of tough fighting. The .45-70 Springfield rifle and carbine played a very important part in all these bloody conflicts.

Custer and his immediate command went under on the Greasy Grass with .45-70 Springfield Carbines and Colt's Peacemakers in their hands and Gibbons command was nearly wiped out in the battle of the Big Hole while using the same weapons.

Throughout this entire period of hard Indian fighting, from the surrender of Chief Joseph of the Nez Perces on the Canadian border to the last roundup of

Apaches in Arizona and Mexico, the .45-70 was the service rifle and carbine cartridge. The cartridge also saw much service in the destruction of the buffalo herds, the Indians' cattle. It was and is a good one, and very deadly on game or man targets. It would break both shoulders of a running Indian pony, or down a huge old buffalo bull when properly placed. Army garrisons scattered throughout the west all carried a supply of .45-70 ammunition, so it was only natural for most commercial gun builders of the period to make and chamber rifles for this great cartridge. The men who used them, both white and red, are now dust and their spirits gone to the Happy Hunting Ground, but the fine old cartridge simply will not die. Modernized with smokeless powder and modern, jacketed, soft-point bullet, when used in good model '86 Winchesters, it is still a prime favorite with timber hunters for all game from deer to grizzly.

For many years Jack Behn has collected and studied .45-70 rifles and carbines. He has used them all in both target shooting and big game hunting, from the single shot carbine to the rare Lowell Battery gun. He knows the cartridge and all arms made for it as few men ever will. He has left no stone unturned to make this the most complete coverage of all arms using the justly famous old cartridge. His observations are accurate and he presents only facts that can be taken at face value. This book represents the work of many years in this one field and is a needed and valuable contribution to Americana.

All collectors of frontier weapons, all big game hunters and students of our Indian wars need this book. They will find completely answered many questions which have plagued them for years. It is a wealth of material, both in description and illustration of .45-70 caliber arms, a finer treatise than anyone else living today could write on the subject. When all of us now existing have crossed the last divide, this book will still be the accepted standard treatise on the .45-70. We all owe Jack Behn a vote of thanks for the production of this great work.

Salmon, Idaho
June 22, 1956   *Elmer Keith*

Contents

	Page
Introduction	xiii
Chapter 1. U. S. Springfield	1
Chapter 2. Winchester	33
Chapter 3. Remington	47
Chapter 4. Bullard	57
Chapter 5. Colt	63
Chapter 6. Sharps	69
Chapter 7. Marlin & Ballard	77
Chapter 8. Peabody & Peabody Martini	89
Chapter 9. Maynard	95
Chapter 10. Whitney	99
Chapter 11. Miscellaneous Makers	107
Chapter 12. Automatic Field Pieces	117
Chapter 13. Handloading the .45-70	129
Appendix	135
Bibliography	137
Schuyler, Hartley & Graham Letter	138

Introduction

MANY VOLUMES on the subject of guns and ammunition adorn the shelves of book stores and libraries throughout the world. There are stories of Colt, Winchester, Smith & Wesson, Sharps and many others, but outside of the .22 rimfire, no book deals with one specific cartridge.

Here the author is endeavoring to relate the story of one of the most famous cartridges ever produced, and of all the guns made to fire it. As for the guns, the text will include those made as standard items of production by regular manufacturers and to some extent little known experimental models.

It has been very difficult to try to find every type and style of firearm adapted to the .45-70 Government cartridge and if the reader is able to stay with this long enough to read it all and knows of some specific arm that has been omitted, the writer would be more than pleased to hear from him.

This book is by no means a single-handed job. Acknowledgment is therefore made to the following for their help: Bill Ruger of Sturm, Ruger & Company; Elmer Keith and C. Mead Patterson of the N.R.A.; to Merrill Deer; John S. duMont; John Hintlian;

George Rowbottom and Phillip Sharpe. To Ed Agromonte, who has helped the author to find many of the rifles described herein.

Also to Thomas Hall of Winchester, Charles Cole of Colt's, C. Gerard Peterson of Remington Arms, and to William Murphy of the Springfield Armory who have made possible many of the photographs contained here, as well as the Lyman Gunsight Company, and Francis Bannerman & Sons.

Others too have added much and I sincerely wish to express my thanks for their help.

Jack Behn

.45-70" RIFLES

CHAPTER 1

U. S. Springfield

THE CIVIL WAR in this country, despite its horrors and tragedies, was actually a great proving ground for firearms. It came at a time when the metallic cartridge was just being developed and breech loading guns were being perfected. Many, many different systems of breech loading carbines were actually used during the war.

At the conclusion of hostilities, the official firearm of the United States was the 1863 Springfield muzzle loading rifle, although many thousands of other kinds of arms were in the hands of troops. The leaders of our armed forces began to look for new and better equipment. Several systems of altering the muzzle loading rifle to breech loading were considered, but the ordnance department decided to use the one designed by Erskine S. Allin, Master Armorer of the Springfield Armory.

Thus was born the Allin conversion in 1865, followed by changes in 1866, 1868, and 1870. The 1865 model was .58 caliber, the rest were of .50 caliber.

The original Allin conversion consisted of milling out the upper section at the rear of the barrel and fixing to the top of it a movable breech block which

Fig. 1. An Officer's Model Springfield rifle being examined by the author. (Note the open "trapdoor.")

would swing forward in the fashion of a trap door. Hence, the nickname "Trapdoor Springfield." Later, a complete receiver was forged with a barrel threaded into it, rather than sweating the butt of the trap door hinge to the top of the barrel. As this type of action is so common, no detailed description is necessary here.

Fig. 1 shows a typical Springfield trapdoor action, with the breech block open (this particular photograph is of an Officer's model).

In 1872 it became evident that the .50 caliber Model 1870 Springfield was not sufficient for field use as it lacked power and range. A board was created by Congress to find a suitable arm for the service. After testing 99 different guns, the board reported favorably on the Springfield (Allins) system. Thus was born the famous .45-70 Springfield.

The following from the Ordnance manual of 1898, gives the details and changes in the Model 1873 U. S. Springfield rifle:

"In pursuance of the Act of Congress approved June 6, 1872, for the purpose of selecting a breech system for the muskets and carbines for the military service of the United States, a Board of Officers composed of Brigadier-General A. H. Terry, U. S. Army; Colonel P. V. Hagner, Ordnance Dept.; Colonel H. B. Clitz, 10th U. S. Infantry; Major M. A. Reno, 7th U. S. Cavalry; and Captain L. L. Livingston, 3rd U. S. Artillery; with Henry Metcalfe, Ordnance Dept., as recorder, was constituted by G. O. No. 58, War Department, A. G. O. June 28, 1872."

During the year 1873 this Board of Officers reported in favor of the "Springfield" system. The minor details as to the caliber form of chamber, ammunition, etc., were determined by a board of ordnance officers convened for that purpose.

Since the adoption of this system the following changes have been made by authority:

Barrel: Rear end of tenon rounded to fit bottom of counterbore in front end of receiver. October, 1878.

Breech Block:
1. Arch filled in, to give greater stiffness to the block. March, 1878.
2. Case-hardened in water. March, 1878.
3. Hinge-pin elongated by broaching instead of reaming. April, 1878.
4. Width increased, October, 1878.
5. Height of comb increased. October, 1878.
6. Angle at front and rear ends of flanges rounded. October, 1878.

Breech-Block Cap: Case-hardening omitted, and cap blackened after fitting. April, 1879.

Breech Screw: Case-hardened in water. March, 1878.

Butt Plate: Made heavier and form changed. August, 1881.

Cam-Latch and Thumb-Piece: Riveted only. End of shaft not ground off to remove riveting marks. June, 1886.

Carbine Band: Band with stacking swivel omitted, and lower band of rifle substituted in the carbine. December, 1879.

Extractor: Lug increased slightly in height. October, 1878.

Firing Pin:
1. Shoulder for firing pin spring omitted, and that portion of pin made conical. Firing pin spring omitted. June, 1878.
2. Firing pins tempered. April, 1879.
3. Slot rounded at corners. January, 1881.
4. To be made hereafter of aluminum bronze, when procurable. December, 1886.

Front Sight:
1. Rifle. A hardened steel sight inserted in the bayonet stud and held by a rivet. July, 1879. Rounded at rear with a radius of 0.15 inches. August, 1887.
2. Carbine. Rear end of hardened front sight made nearly vertical instead of beveled. January, 1880.
3. Front sights for new model arms made higher and thinner. .653 inches for rifles, .738 inches for carbines, height above axis of bore. September, 1885.
4. Carbine. Made same thickness above stud as that for rifle. November, 1889.
5. Carbine. Height of front sight made .728 inches. December, 1890.

Front Sight Cover: Detachable; first issued October, 1883; made component part of arm March, 1886.
New model, for rifle and carbine, approved February, 1888. Carbine front sight cover modified and secured by a pin. December, 1890.

Hammer: Lip placed on under side of head. January, 1880.

Hinge Pin: Lengthened to correspond with altered receiver. October, 1878.

Lower Band: Top surface grooved to accommodate it to rear sight. Model 1884.

Main Spring Swivel Rivets: Tempered instead of being left soft. April, 1880.

Ramrod Stop: Drawn to spring temper, and angle reinforced slightly. August, 1879.

Rear Sight:

Model 1887 differed from previous models in number and position of graduation marks, shape of sighting notch, etc. First form, with offsets on base. January, 1877. Second form, with curve of base continuous. May, 1878.

Model 1879, "buckhorn," differed from previous models in having a buckhorn-shaped eye-piece attached to the slide, and in the slide, which can be moved laterally to correct the aim for wind, drift, and errors of construction of piece.

FIRST FORM. Graduation marks for windage placed .02 inches apart, and with projecting points on lower edge of buckhorn plate. January, 1879.

SECOND FORM:
1. Graduation marks for windage, placed .04 inches apart.
2. Projecting points on lower edge of buckhorn plate cut off.
3. Centering pin notch in buckhorn plate made wide, "V"-shaped.
4. Upper edge of buckhorn plate made straight, with a large semicircular notch. October, 1879.

THIRD FORM. Upper surface of hinge of leaf "flattened." November, 1879.

FOURTH FORM:

1. Form of notch on lower edge of buckhorn plate for centering pin made semicircular.
2. Large notch between buckhorns made straight at bottom, instead of rounded and beveled toward the front. July, 1880.

MODEL 1884. This sight has been modified as follows since its first issue:

1. Heads of windage and bindings screws enlarged to give more power to fingers and to overlap sides of leaf when down, in order to give leaf lateral support.
2. Action of binding screw on slide changed to hold it more firmly.
3. Movable base and slide case-hardened. August, 1886. Rear-sight protector band, for carbines, approved October, 1890.

Receiver:

1. Width increased the whole length. October, 1878.
2. Thickness of metal on top of front end increased. October, 1878.
3. All re-entrant angles and bottom of counterbore for tennon of barrel rounded. October, 1878.
4. Gas escapes on sides made deeper and extended farther towards rear. October, 1878.

Rod Bayonet Rifle: Experimental, issued for trial January, 1886. Final model, known as model 1888, approved February, 1890.

Sear: Nose thickened. January, 1885. Angle of sear changed to prevent nose from catching on edge of safety notch. August, 1886.

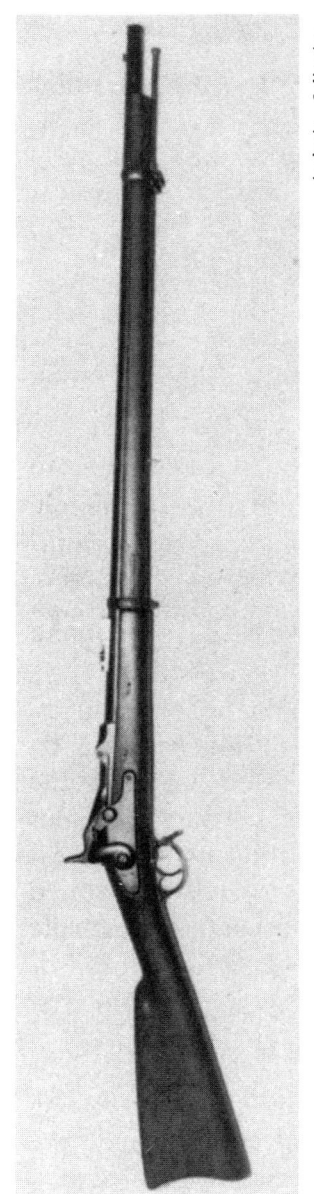 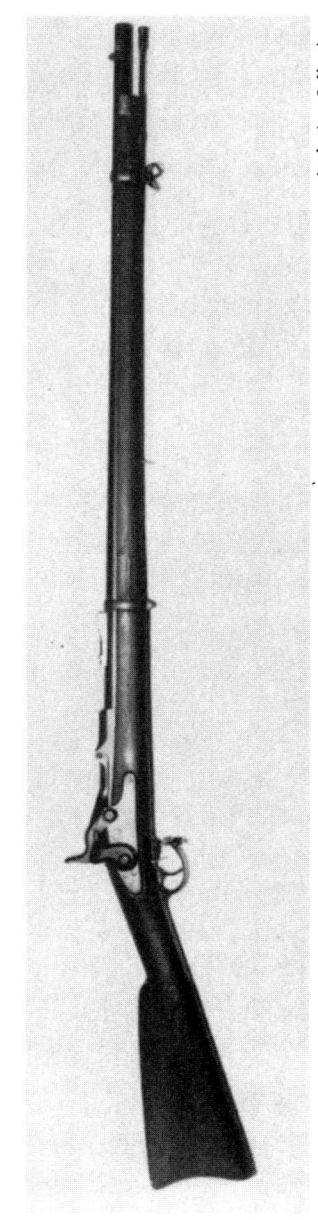

Fig. 2. U. S. Springfield—a mutation made of parts, i.e.: 1863 lock, 1868 receiver, 1869 breech block. *Author's Collection*

Fig. 3. Another mutation with 1863 lock and 1870 breech block. *Author's Collection*

Stock:
1. Hole bored under front end of guard plate, to intersect ramrod groove at its lower end and facilitate removal of dirt when collected at bottom of groove. April, 1879.
2. Rear end of barrel groove slightly widened and deepened to receive enlarged receiver. October, 1878.

Trigger: Straight corrugated trigger adopted March, 1883.

Thumb piece: Underside of firing pin guard cut away to the end of the guard, instead of being notched. March, 1876. Cut away to prevent striking lock plate. January, 1883.

Tumbler: Notches of tumbler widened to correspond with thickened nose of sear. January, 1885.

After having just read the large number of changes, that is official changes, made by the Ordnance Department in the '73 Springfield and then add to those the number of unofficial changes made in the field, plus some (not all by any means) dealers who like to assemble rifles, it is not hard to believe when it is stated that a true and complete Model 1873 Springfield rifle as issued is indeed hard to find. Guns assembled of many models are common as is shown here in the first few photographs.

The following illustrates combinations incorporating changes of different years.

The U. S. Springfield serial number 10442, caliber .45-70, Fig. 2, proves the above as the main parts on it

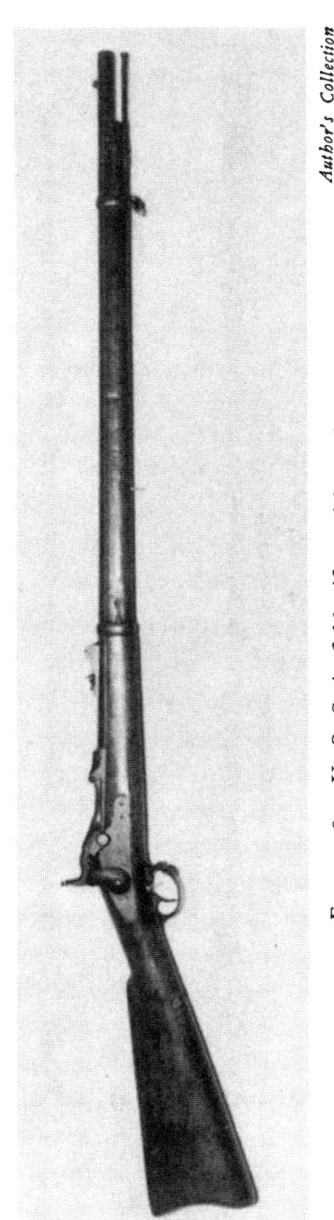

Fig. 4. 1873 U. S. Springfield rifle, serial number 68567.

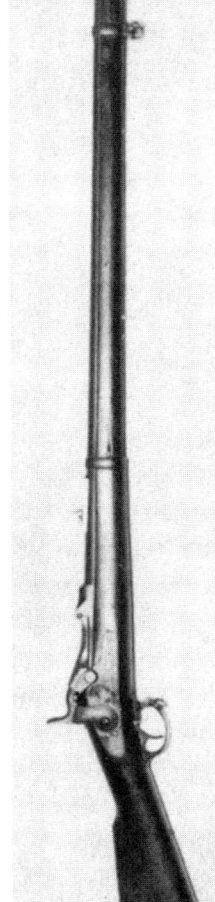

Fig. 5. 1879 U. S. Springfield rifle, serial number 369950.

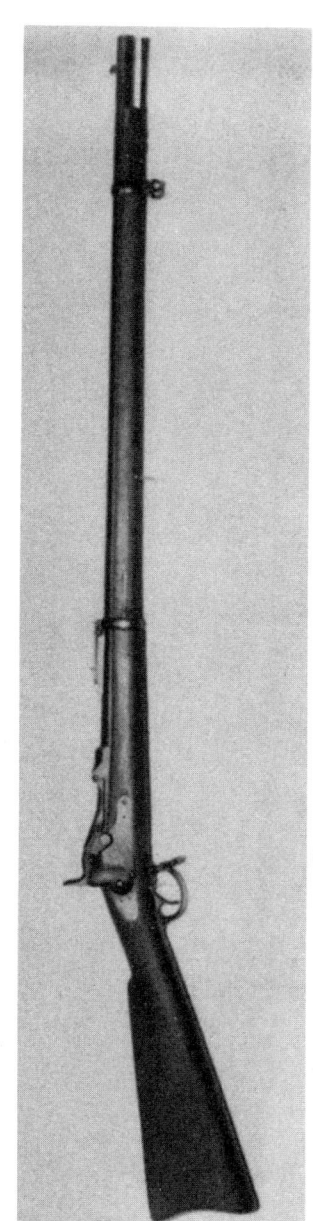

Fig. 6. 1879 U. S. Springfield rifle, serial number 325360 with Buffington rear sight of 1884 added.

Author's Collection

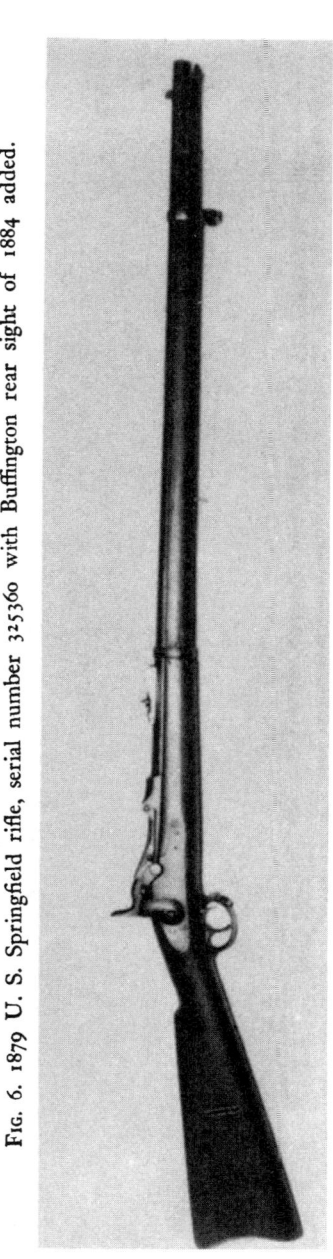

Fig. 7. 1880 experimental U. S. Springfield rifle, serial number 157188 with triangular ramrod bayonet.

Author's Collection

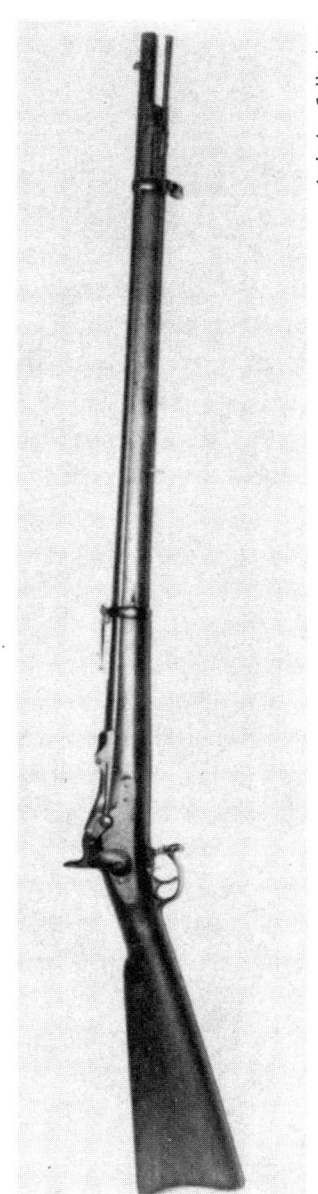#
FIG. 8. 1884 U. S. Springfield rifle, serial number 390011.

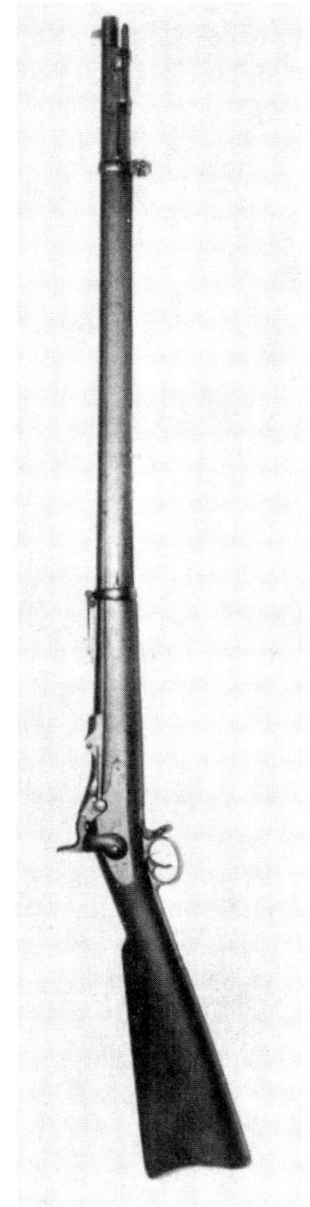
FIG. 9. 1888 U. S. Springfield rifle, serial number 514336.

are as follows: lock 1863, receiver 1868, breech block marked 1869, and a .45-70 model 1873 barrel—truly a mutation.

The U. S. Springfield serial number 122634, caliber .45-70, Fig. 3, has a lock which is 1863 and a breech block of 1870. All other parts 1873.

The U. S. Springfield, serial number 68567, caliber .45-70, Fig. 4, is definitely a model of 1873 with the exception that the rear sight has been replaced with the 1879 model.

U. S. Springfield serial number 369950 caliber .45-70, Fig. 5, is the model 1879 with improvements added as per the manual previously listed.

U. S. Springfield serial number 325360 caliber .45-70, Fig. 6, is another model 1879 with the exception of the Buffington rear sight.

In about 1880 approximately 1000 experimental model Springfield rifles were made the same as model 1879, with the exception that a triangular ramrod bayonet was substituted for the conventional cleaning rod. This rifle is shown in Fig. 7. The Springfield serial number is 157188.

U. S. Springfield serial number 390011. The model 1884 is shown in Fig. 8. The main change from model 1879 is the famous Buffington rear sight with a worm gear for windage adjustment.

The three pieces pictured in Figs. 9, 10 and 11 are peculiar in their similarity, all being model 1888 (or 1889 as some authorities call them) have relatively close serial numbers, and inspector stamps of 1891.

This model had two major changes over the '84, in that the trigger guard was now made in one piece, that

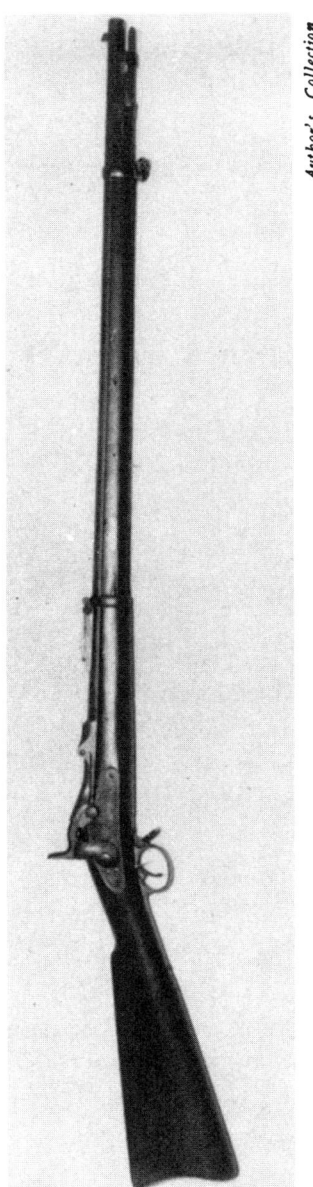

FIG. 10. 1888 U. S. Springfield rifle, serial number 512131.

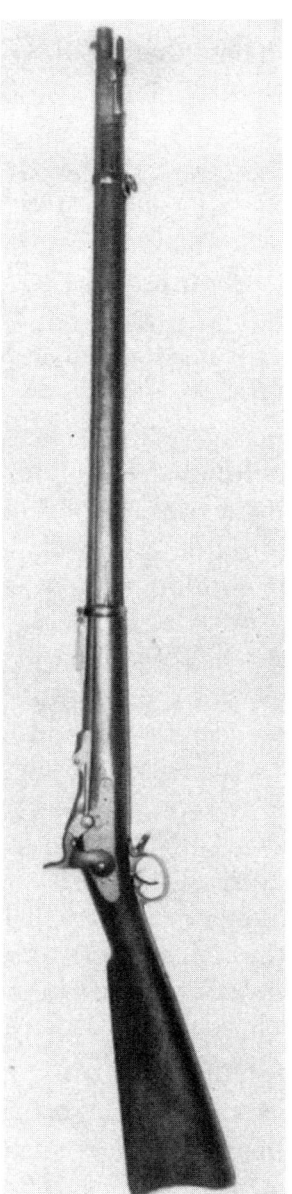

FIG. 11. 1888 U. S. Springfield rifle, serial number 515764.

14

is the loop was not screwed on as in previous models, and it had the round ramrod bayonet.

With this we have the last single shot rifle used by our government.

The U. S. Springfield Rifle, serial number 470082, Fig. 12, was obtained from Joseph Van Dorn of Valley Center, Calif., in 1951 and is pictured just as received.

It is noted that besides having the single prong Schuetzen butt plate and double set triggers, there is a block in place of the front sight. At the end of the tang is an inlet where a receiver sight was fitted, also forward of the trigger guard is a second inlet to accommodate a palm rest. Another interesting feature on this arm is a stop that holds the breech block from passing the vertical position and tapped holes forward of the receiver which could indicate that at one time it had either a scope or a sighting tube.

This is a fine example of a target rifle made from a military.

The cadet model U. S. Springfield had a 29½ inch barrel. All other dimensions were the same as the rifle. Fig. 13 is an 1873 model, serial number 336319, with the Buffington sight added and with sling swivels which are not regular equipment.

Fig. 14, serial number 416772, Model 1884 has the sling swivels. The cadet model was used by the Navy as they did not like the size of the regular rifle, it being awkward, yet they did not approve of the carbine.

Along with the Colt Frontier, the Springfield carbine ranks high in the winning of the West, as it was the standard arm for the famous U. S. Cavalry.

In the book, *Firearms in the Custer Battle*, by John E.

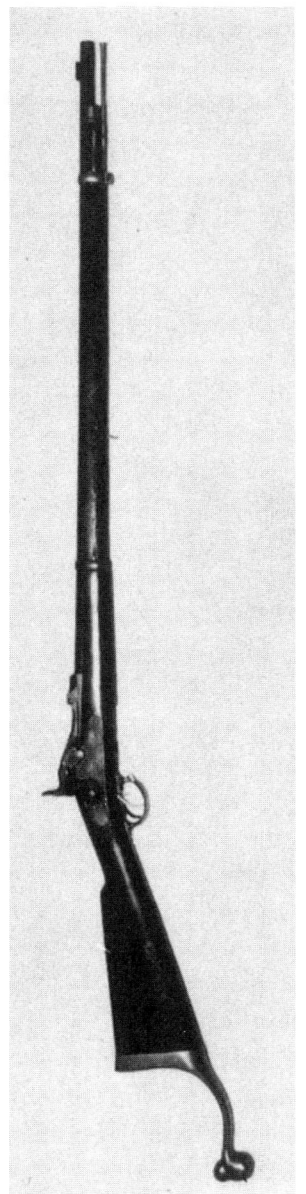

FIG. 12. A Springfield Model 1884 rebuilt into a Schuetzen type target rifle with double set triggers. *Author's Collection*

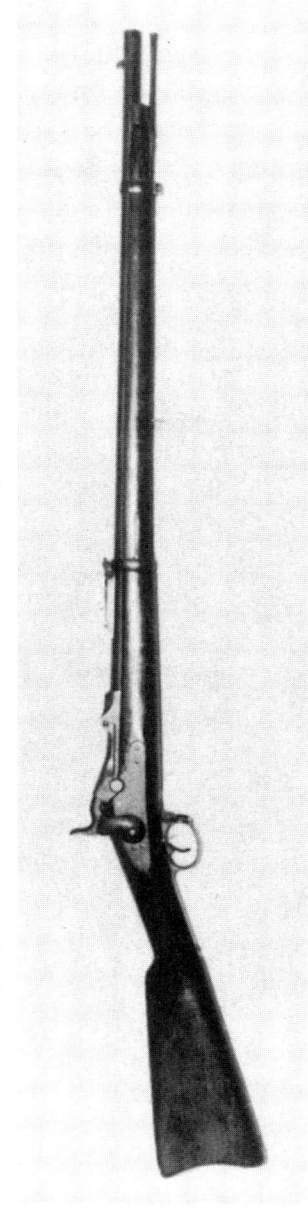

FIG. 13. 1873 U. S. Springfield Cadet rifle, serial number 336319. *Author's Collection*

Parsons and John S. duMont, there is a summary of the arms inventory of all but four companies (from which there were no returns) of the 7th cavalry.

The list shows the .45-70 carbine was the standard weapon of the 7th along with, of course, the .45 Colt S. A. army revolver.

The carbine differs from the rifle basically in the shorter stock and a barrel length of 22 inches. The cleaning rod for the carbine is in three pieces and it is carried under the butt plate along with a headless shell extractor.

Pictured, Fig. 15, is serial number 181842, which is from all appearances an 1879 model. Fig. 16, serial number 342947 is evidently another 1879 with the Buffington sight added; Fig. 17, serial number 147442, is truly of the 1884 variety with the barrel band of 1890 added.

It is here noted that in almost all of the Springfield described in these pages, the serial numbers and model variations seem to have no consistency, again indicating ordnance depots making changes on arms turned in by troops.

Of all the arms ever made available to the U. S. Armed forces, it is the author's opinion that one of the most highly prized, bar none, including the early Harpers Ferry models, is the "Officer's model Springfield Model 1875."

The best written description of it is given in the Springfield Manual:

Springfield rifle, officer's model 1875. The weight of this rifle is about 8 pounds, varying with the density of the wood used in the stock. The length of the barrel is 26 inches. The stock is checkered "fore and aft" the breech, and is tipped with white metal. The rifle has a

Author's Collection

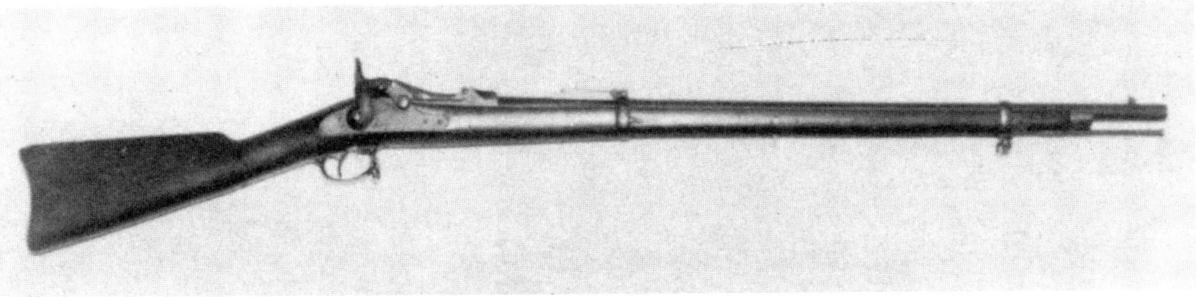

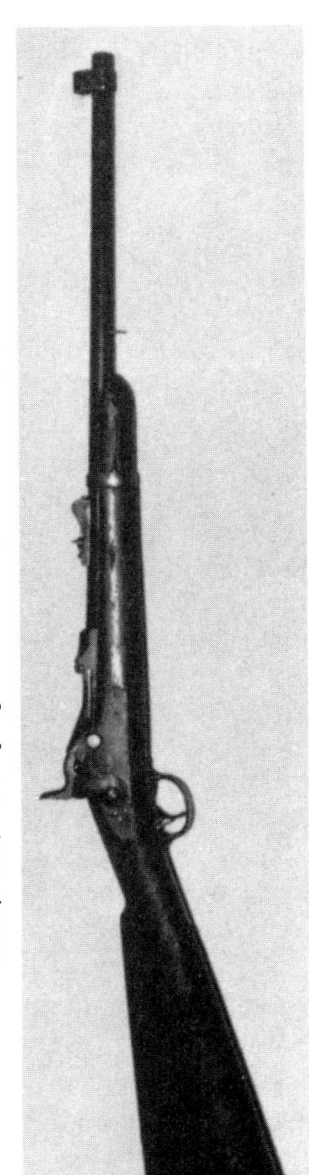

FIG. 14. 1884 U. S. Springfield Cadet rifle, serial number 416772.

Author's Collection

FIG. 15. 1879 U. S. Springfield carbine, serial number 181842.

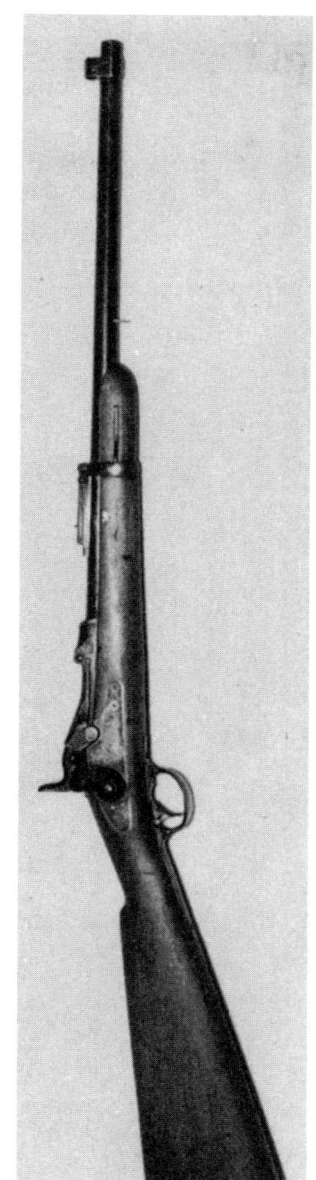

Fig. 16. 1884 U. S. Springfield carbine, serial number 342947.

Fig. 17. 1884 U. S. Springfield carbine, serial number 147442 with the 1890 barrel band.

plain "buckhorn" sight on the barrel, graduated like the service sight, and also has peep and globe sights. The globe sight can be folded down on the barrel, when its pin becomes an open front sight, to be used with the buckhorn sight. The peep has a lateral as well as vertical motion, and by turning the screw and loosening, it may be adjusted to counteract any diviation to the right or left. When at the bottom of the slide the peep is adjusted for a range of 50 yards; when at the top it is adjusted for a range of 1,100 yards. The peep sight may be folded down on the stock either forward or backward. In the former position the peep should be pushed to the bottom of the slide, or the hammer, in being cocked, will strike it.

The globe sight is a considerable distance from the buckhorn and peep sights, 20.8 inches and 32.75 inches respectively.

The rifle has a "Single-set" trigger. When set, it is a hair trigger; when unset, it is the ordinary service trigger, requiring a pull of 6-8 pounds. The trigger should be set by pushing forward with the thumb after cocking the hammer—never before. A "Fly" in the tumbler carries the sear over the half-cock notch when the trigger is set.

The ramrod is of wood, both ends being ferruled with brass, nickel-plated. The ferrule on the smaller end has a slot for the admission of a wiping-rag; that on the larger end has a milled head for convenience in drawing out the rod. A small pin in the underside of the barrel, entering a hole in the rod just below this milled head, prevents the rod from slipping out of place. The breech-block, receiver, hammer, lock, band, and the heel of the butt-plate are all plainly engraved.

The cost of the rifle is $27.00; screwdriver $.17, packing box $1.50.

The description and dimensions of the parts of the rifle, other than those above mentioned, are the same as of the corresponding parts of the Springfield rifle.

NOTE: All officers' rifles made after April, 1877, have a detachable pistol-grip handle; and the peep sight as the buckhorn sight is graduated with approximate accuracy for the Frankford rifle cartridge. The lowest elevation on both sights corresponds to 50 yard range.

Fig. 18 pictures 1875 Officer's Model Springfield. This rifle belonging to Mr. William B. Ruger of Southport, Connecticut, is evidently one of the first manufactured as it has the original 1873 breech block with the high arch.

This piece bears neither a serial number nor an inspector's stamp.

Fig. 19 pictures an officer's model which according to the inspector's stamp was produced in 1881. As noted above, this specimen being manufactured after 1877 has the detachable pistol grip. On the receiver forward of the tang appears the figures 1881.

As most similar models bear no serial number, it is believed that this number is a date of manufacture as it corresponds to the same date as the inspector's stamp.

This rifle pictured in Fig. 20 is one of the most prized pieces in the author's collection. This Officer's Model, as the inspector's stamp shows, was made in 1885 and is in mint condition throughout. As stated above no serial number appears at all.

A third type of Officer's Model which is extremely rare is illustrated in Fig. 21. As the picture shows, on

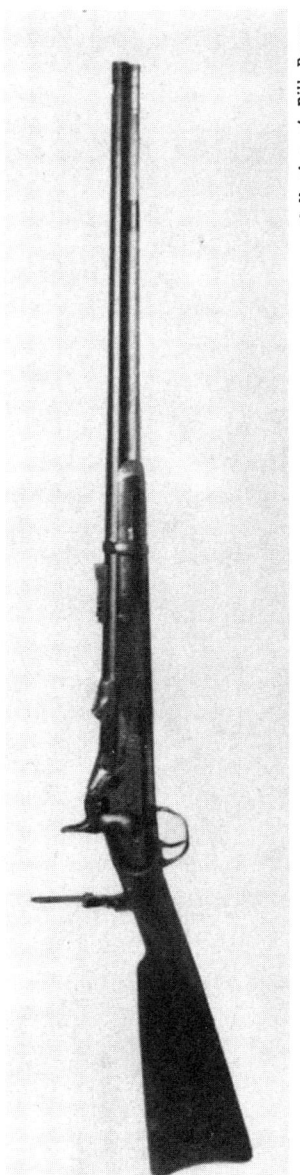 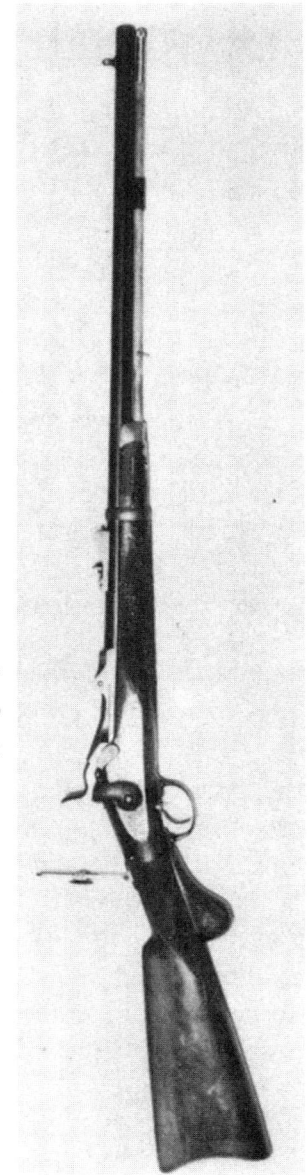

FIG. 18. 1875 Springfield Officer's model 1st type. *Collection of Bill Ruger*

FIG. 19. 1875 Springfield Officer's model 2nd type. *Author's Collection*

22

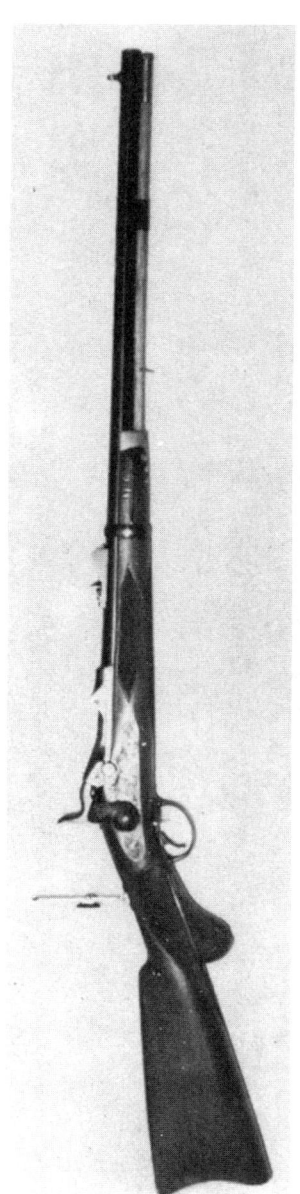

Author's Collection

FIG. 20. 1875 Springfield Officer's model 2nd type.

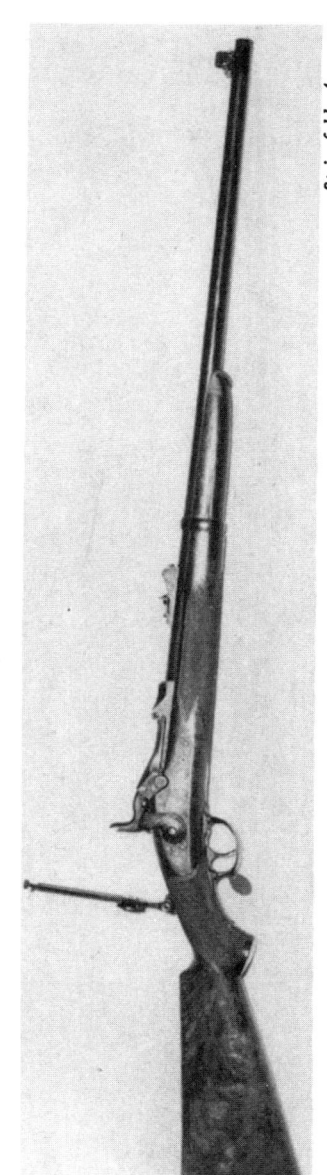

Springfield Armory

FIG. 21. 1875 Springfield Officer's model 3rd type.

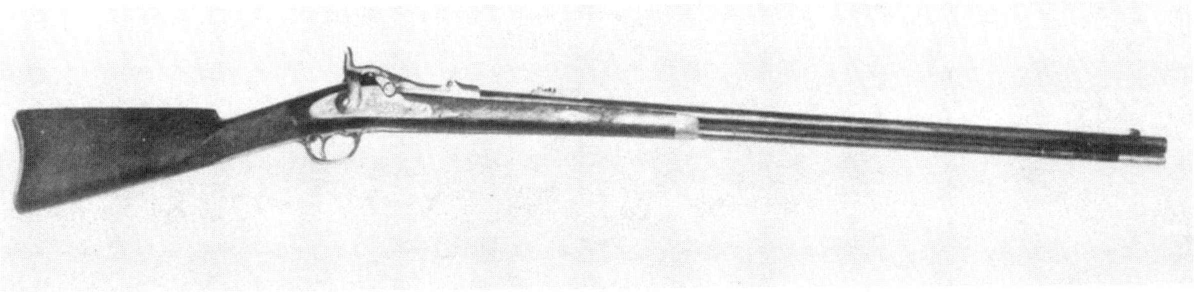

FIG. 22. Special Springfield Officer's model, serial number 14210. Relic of Custer's battle. *Springfield Armory*

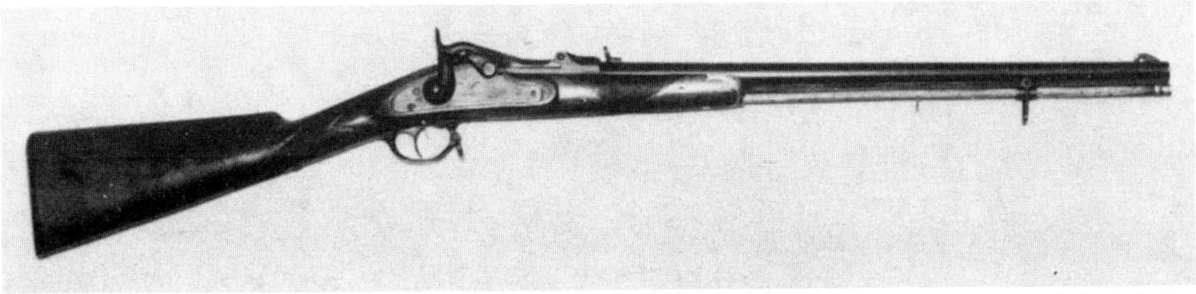

FIG. 23. Counterfeit of Springfield Officer's model. *Author's Collection*

this version there is an integral pistol grip and the usual cleaning rod under the barrel has been placed in the butt stock as on the carbine, and a globe front sight with windage adjustment added.

While visiting at the Springfield Arsenal Museum, I came upon an Officer's Model which had a 32½ inch barrel and an overall length of 52 inches. Every other detail checked with the correct description. Inquiring into the card file at the museum, it was learned that the rifle was listed as a "Special" Officer's Model. The specimen bears the serial number 14210, as a serial number as stated before is unusual on an Officer's Model. A further note on the index card states the piece as a "Relic of the Custer Battle at Little Big Horn." The gun is shown in Fig. 22.

As will happen to most collectors, sometimes they will get a forgery. Fig. 23 shows a converted Springfield rifle, serial number 37979, which was passed off as an Officer's Model by a dealer. It is believed that after talking with the dealer, he himself did not know the difference, but upon close examination, it is easily distinguishable, as no dimensions check. There is no engraving and the standard service trigger is used. Regardless of this, it shows what can be done to a military rifle if someone puts the time to it.

As a final note on the single shot Springfield rifle, it seems necessary to include a partial listing of the experimental magazines that were submitted in the trials of 1872. These magazines were an effort to have a supply of fresh cartridges ready for loading into the single shot rifle. Fig. 24 shows Colonel Benton's fixed magazine; it holds five shells and is an integral part of the stock. Col. Benton's magazine is so arranged that when the breech

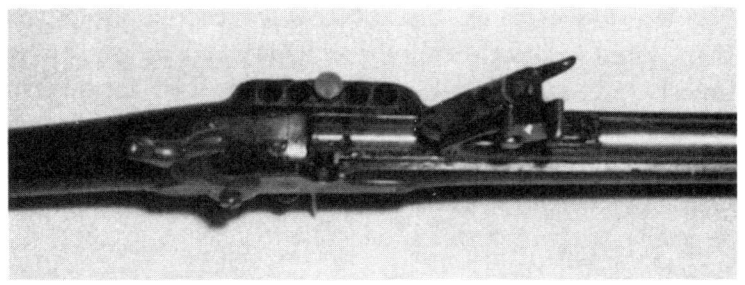

Springfield Armory

FIG. 24. Colonel Benton's fixed magazine.

block was closed, it overlapped the rim of the cartridges holding them in place and keeping them from falling out.

Lieut. Metcalfe's plan (Fig. 25) was to attach a box of 10 cartridges to the side of the rifle. These illustrations are only two of nine submitted in these tests.

The Lee single shot rifle can be described here as it was made at the Springfield Armory under the supervision of James Paris Lee of Stevens Point, Wisconsin, the inventor who came to Springfield for this purpose.

In 1874 Congress appropriated $10,000.00, for the manufacture of these arms. All records show only 143 were made. The tang of the receiver was marked "U. S. Pat. March 16, 1875."

The action is described by Gluckman in his book, *U. S. Muskets Rifles & Carbines*, as follows:

The dropping breech-block mechanism was operated by striking the hammer forward with the heel of the hand to depress the breech and open the chamber for loading. When the cartridge was inserted, its rim moved the extractor back, which, when fully seated, raised the breech into firing position by action of the two-leaf mainspring, one of the leaves operating the hammer and the other the breech-block. The piece was fired by a conventional center hammer. The action had the disadvantage of difficulty of closure unless a shell was used to trip the extractor. Another disadvantage was necessity of having the hammer at half or full cock to assure positive locking of the breech-block.

A picture of the Lee rifle is shown in Fig. 26.

It seems that there was only one repeating rifle in .45-70 marked "U.S. Springfield" and made completely at the Armory. This was the Chaffee-Reese or the "U.S. Springfield 1884 Chaffee-Reese."

The arm was invented by Mr. R. S. Chaffee and General J. N. Reese of Springfield, Illinois, and was

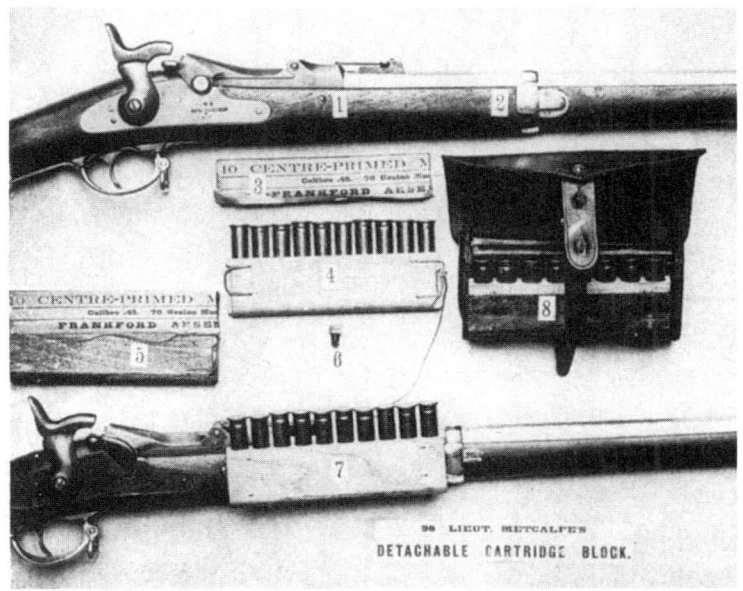

Springfield Armory

FIG. 25. Lieutenant Metcalfe's detachable magazine.

27

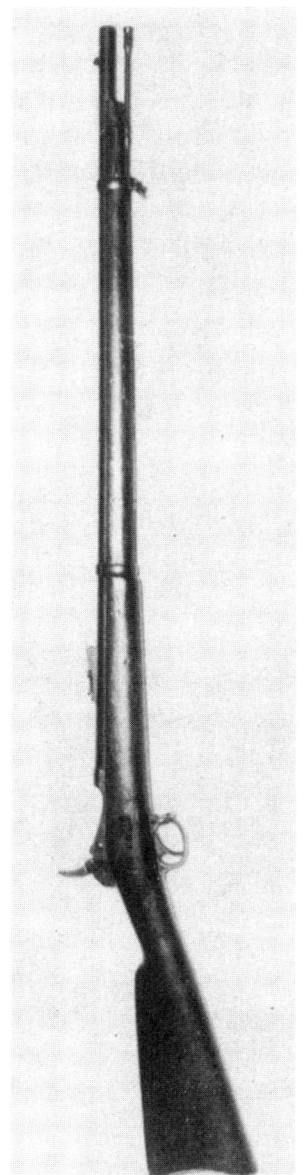

Fig. 26. Lee single shot rifle. *Springfield Armory*

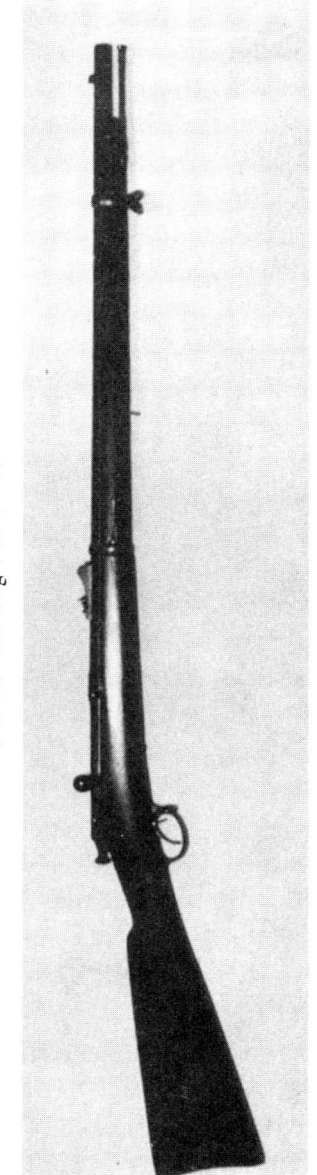

Fig. 27. Chaffee-Reese rifle. *Author's Collection*

approved by the Ordnance Board of 1882, appointed for the Selection of a Magazine arm for our service.

The action was of the turnbolt type. The forward motion of the bolt caused a cartridge from a magazine in the butt stock to be fed forward into the chamber. A pair of ratchet bars in the magazine fed the cartridges into action in front of the bolt face, yet the same bars keep the shells from touching each other in the magazine to prevent accidental discharge.

Loading is accomplished through a trap door in the butt plate. Seven hundred fifty-three Chaffee-Reese rifles were made in the Springfield Armory in 1884.

The rifle in Fig. 27 bears no serial number.

At this point, the Ward-Burton rifle deserves mention. Although Ward-Burton rifles numbering slightly over 1,000 were made at Springfield and put into the hands of our troops for field trial, these were chambered for the .50-70 cartridge. I find no record of it being made in .45 caliber in any quantity. Fig. 28 illustrates a repeating rifle in .45 caliber which is on display in the Springfield Armory, probably purely experimental. This specimen is a magazine rifle with the magazine in the butt stock as in the Chaffee-Reese.

Phil Sharpe also mentions a Ward-Burton "commercial" rifle in our caliber. It is described as a "bolt action type with a Magazine built to hold three to eight cartridges. The weight of this rifle, depending upon the magazine size ran from 8 to 10 pounds."

At this point, we come to the conclusion of the rifles made in .45-70 government caliber, at the Springfield Armory. All guns described so far with the exception of the note on the commercial Ward-Burton, were made in Springfield. Those made by the Government

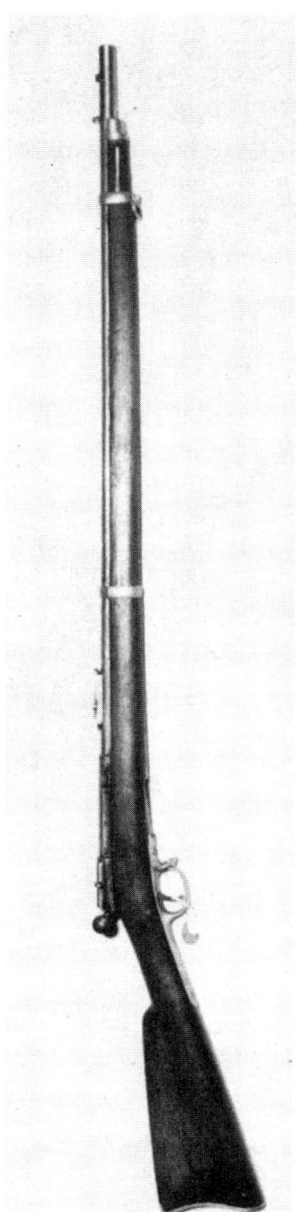

FIG. 28. Ward-Burton rifle. *Springfield Armory*

30

are actually only a small portion of the guns manufactured in this caliber.

We will now, in the following chapters describe and discuss those made commercially. The order of the following chapters bear no significance as to the importance of their makers.

CHAPTER 2

Winchester

THE READERS of this volume will probably need no details about Winchester's history. As for the subject, the .45-70 cartridge, Winchester's contributions were many.

One of the best known was the famous single shot which was made from 1885 until 1920. This was produced in most caliber, from .22 short to the .50-95 express. The variations of barrel lengths and weights, as well as types and grades of stocks were almost unlimited. The basic action was a lever-type falling block construction.

Some of the models made for the lighter calibers had the side wall of the receiver partially cut away; but the ones used for the heavier calibers, such as .45-70, were called "High Side Walls," as the breech-block was fully supported by the side of the action.

The model pictured in Fig. 29 is the military musket version. It bears the serial number 2483 and according to Winchester was shipped from the factory May 24, 1886.

In checking further with Mr. Thomas Hall of the Winchester Museum, it was learned that even though the 1885 Single Shot was chambered for so many differ-

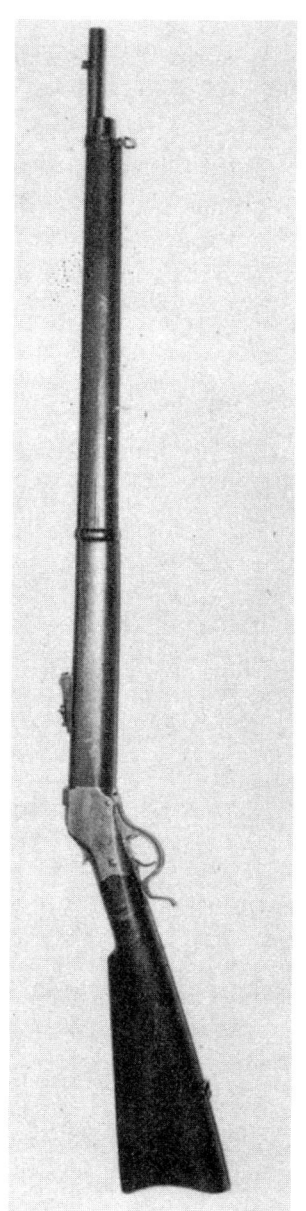

FIG. 29. Winchester single shot rifle, serial number 2483. (Military musket version) Shipped from factory, May 24, 1886.

Author's Collection

FIG. 30. 1879 Hotchkiss carbine, serial number 4368. Shipped from factory July 27, 1883.

Author's Collection

ent cartridges, Winchester's records show that serial number 2 was a .45-70, and that serial number 9 was the first .45-70 caliber Musket.

The first true bolt action rifle ever produced on this continent was Winchester's Hotchkiss. Mr. B. B. Hotchkiss brought this arm from France and exhibited it at the Centennial Exposition in Philadelphia where it was seen by Winchester, who purchased it within the year.

The Hotchkiss rifle was of bolt action variety and had a 6 shot magazine in the butt stock which was loaded with the bolt open by inserting the shell in the open action and pushing it backwards down into the magazine in the stock.

Pictured here in Figs. 30, 31 and 32 are two military carbines and one musket of the 1879 model. The carbines are serial numbers 4368 and 16316, which were shipped from the factory on July 27, 1883 and July 27, 1882, respectively. The musket is new and is in the Winchester Museum collection. Serial number 15203 has never left the Winchester factory.

A new model Hotchkiss was introduced in 1883. On this version a solid steel receiver was used with a two piece stock. The general operation of the rifle was the same as the 1879 model; a magazine cut-off was placed on the side of the rifle. The 1883 model was produced as a military rifle, military carbine and sporting rifle. Fig. 33 shows a military rifle, serial number 80956, which was assembled at Winchester, February, 1895.

A standard sporting model is shown in Fig. 34. This bears the serial number 52786 and was shipped February 5, 1886.

A very highly decorated and engraved sporting rifle,

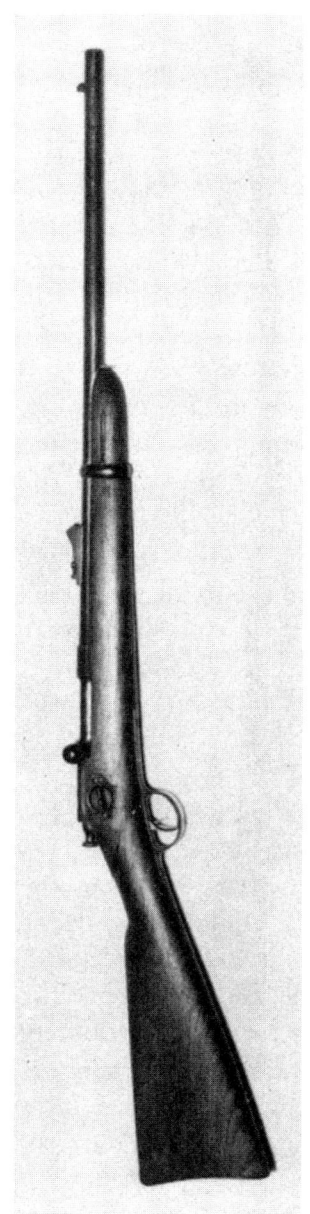

FIG. 31. 1879 Hotchkiss carbine, serial number 16316. Shipped July 27, 1882.

Author's Collection

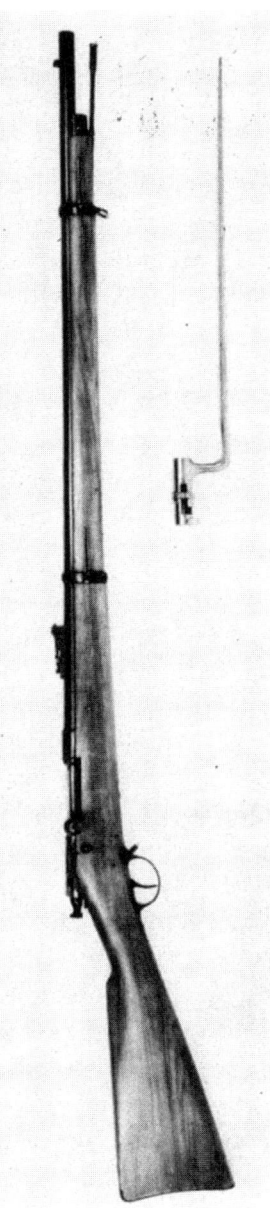

FIG. 32. 1879 Hotchkiss military rifle, serial number 15203.

Courtesy of Winchester-Western Division Olin Mathieson Chemical Corporation

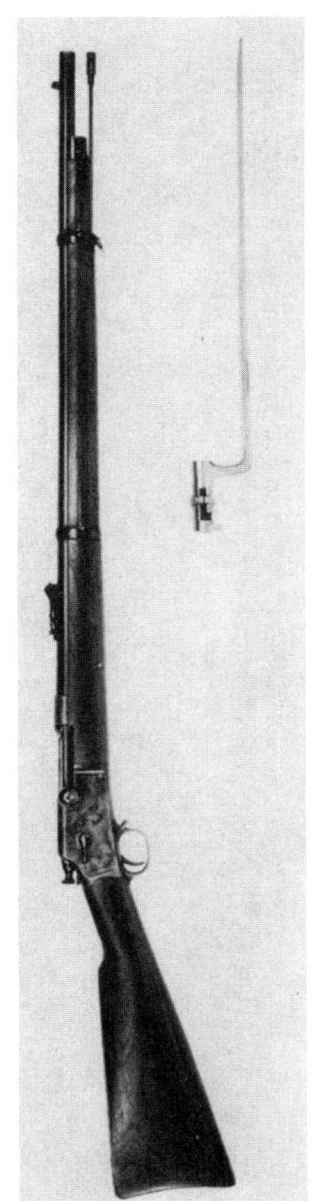

Courtesy of Winchester-Western Division Olin Mathieson Chemical Corporation

FIG. 33. 1883 Hotchkiss rifle, serial number 80956. Assembled February, 1895.

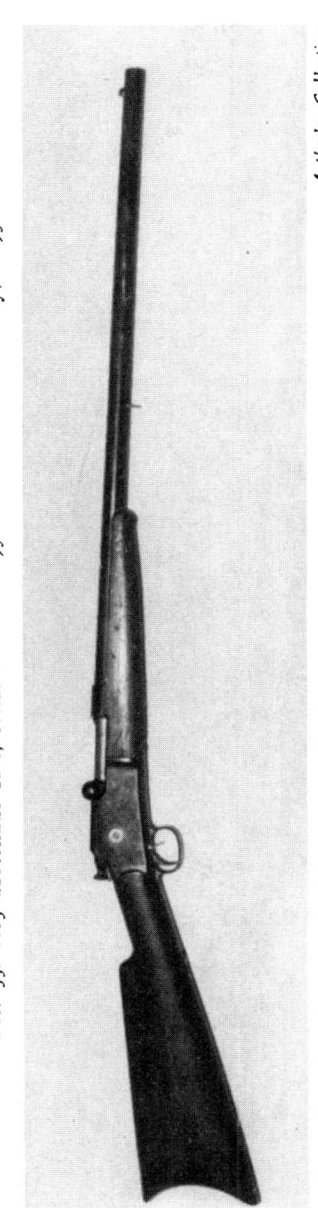

Author's Collection

FIG. 34. 1883 Hotchkiss Sporting rifle, serial number 52786.

FIG. 35. A very fancy 1883 Hotchkiss Sporting rifle, serial number 52708.

Courtesy of Winchester-Western Division Olin Mathieson Chemical Corporation

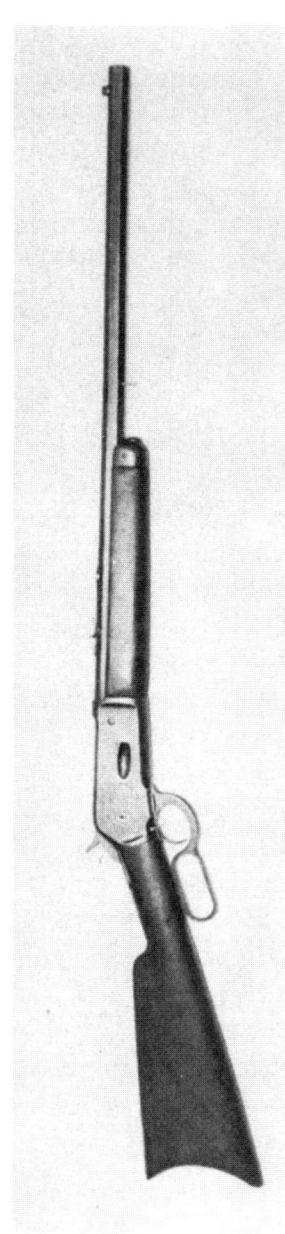

FIG. 36. An 1886 Winchester 26 inch octagon barrel, ½ magazine, serial number 50662.

Author's Collection

which is now in the Winchester Museum is shown in Fig. 35. This rifle was assembled February 8, 1888, and marked with serial number 52708.

For 49 years Winchester produced the model 1886 lever action repeater. Although this model was chambered for 10 different cartridges it is worthy to note here that it was the first introduced in 1886 to handle the .45-70.

Of all the lever action rifles made, none have compared to the '86 for ease and smoothness of operation. The movement of the lever to operate the action was practically effortless.

The first announcement of this model introduced in October, 1886, stated that it had a 26 inch barrel available in either round, octagon, or half octagon. The full length tubular magazine held 8 cartridges, and with one in the chamber it made a 9 shot gun. A half-magazine version was also available as well as fancy models which had case hardened trimmings, pistol grip, and shotgun butt stock. In 1894, the '86 was announced available in a take-down style.

Probably the two versions of the model being discussed here, which still hold much popularity even today are the light weight 22 inch round nickel steel barrel, full or half magazine, with shotgun rubber butt plate and blued finish model, and the carbine.

The lightweight number weighed 6¾ pounds. The carbine was furnished with a 22 inch barrel also, but had only a full magazine available. The trimmings were case hardened, and when weighed it tipped the scales at 7¾ pounds.

A take-down carbine could be had the same as above, but it weighed 7¼ pounds.

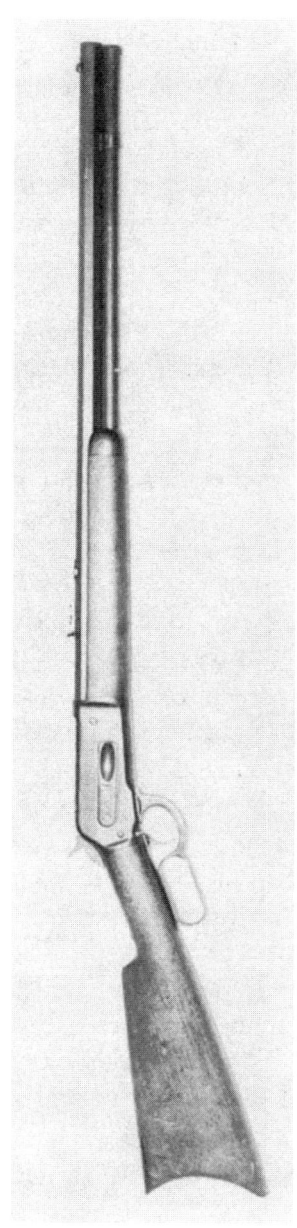

Fig. 37. An 1886 Winchester 26 inch octagon barrel, full magazine, serial number 28851.

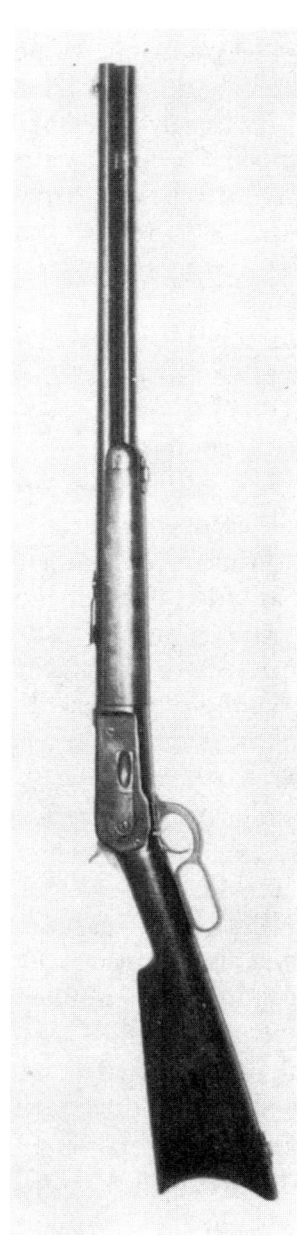

Fig. 38. An 1886 Winchester 26 inch round barrel, full magazine, serial number 20893.

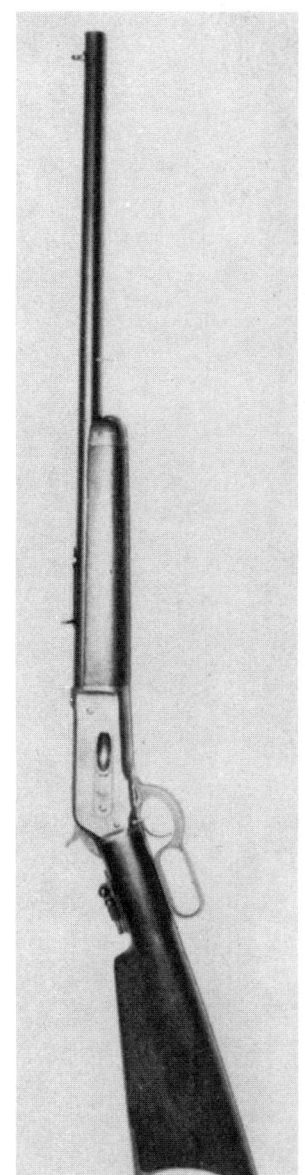

Fig. 39. An 1886 Winchester 26 inch round barrel, ½ magazine, serial number 67788. *Author's Collection*

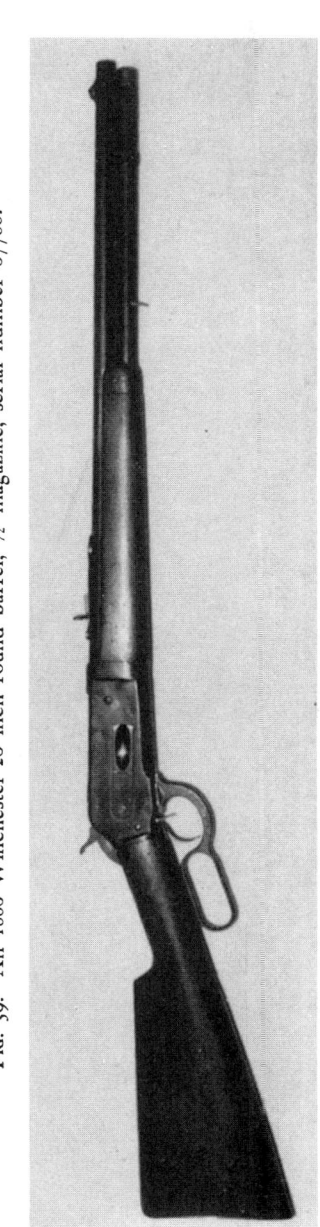

Fig. 40. An 1886 Winchester light weight, take down model, serial number 149200. *Author's Collection*

FIG. 41. An 1886 Winchester light weight, solid frame model, serial number 130757.
Author's Collection

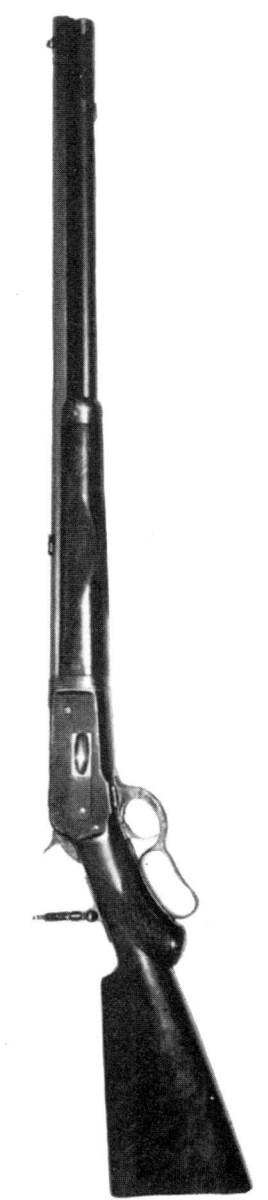

FIG. 42. An 1886 Winchester take down rifle with pistol grip.
Merrill Deer Collection

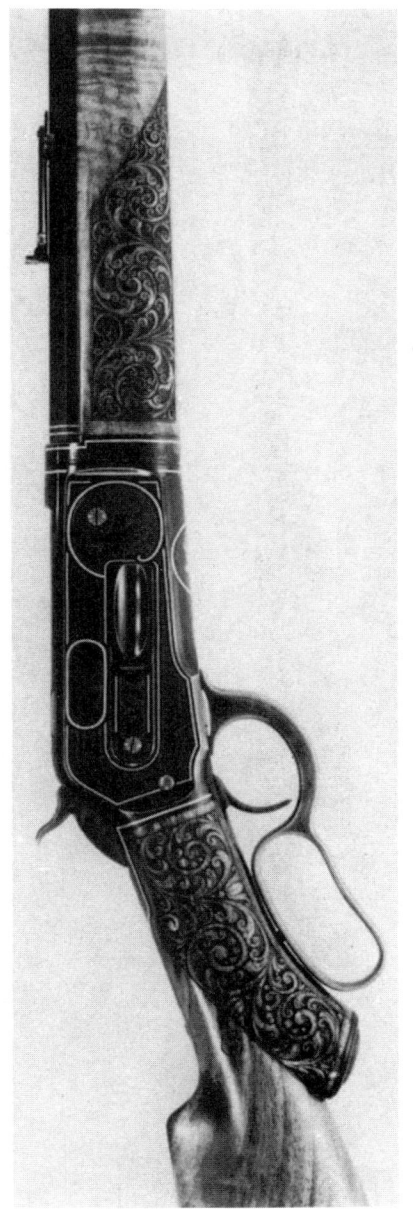

Fig. 43. A really dressed up '86 Winchester.

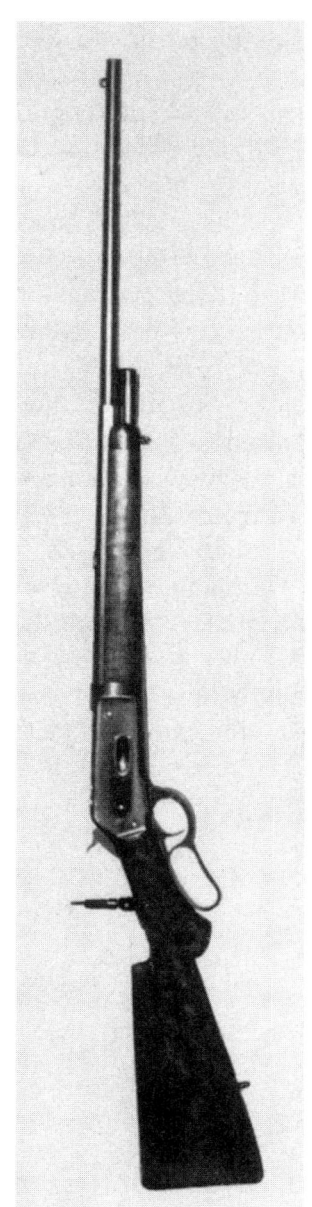

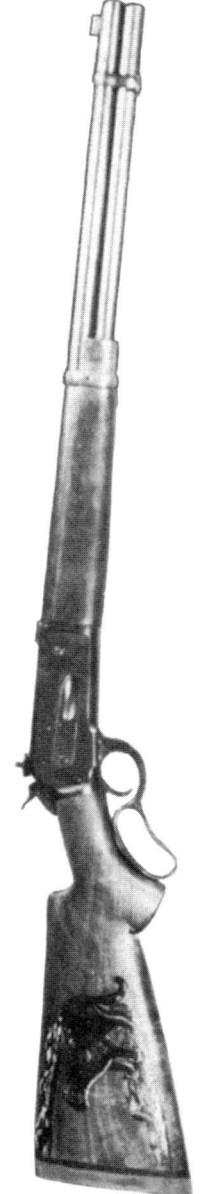

FIG. 44. Another fancy '86.

FIG. 45. Elmer Keith's '86 carbine. Rebarrelled and stocked by Hughel's Gun Shop, Monroe, Washington.

In 49 years of production, Winchester made over 160,000 model 1886 rifles.

Pictured are some of the author's '86 Winchesters.

Probably the finest of the fancy grade Winchesters, which was made for a British Exposition, is shown in Fig. number 43, and is numbered 119732. According to Winchester, it was assembled September 5, 1899 and is marked to have style "A" carving at a cost of $60.00. Style "1" engraving, cost, without the gold inlays, $250.00. This gun bears British proof-marks.

Another fancy grade '86, which is owned by Bill Ruger, is shown in Fig. 44. This one has 26 inch half-octagon barrel, with the take-down feature and has an extra .50-100 barrel. Serial number on this gun is 12035, which was shipped October 18, 1899.

Down through the years one of the biggest boosters of the .45-70 cartridge for big game at short range, has been Elmer Keith. Elmer was kind enough to forward to me a picture of his favorite '86, which is shown in Fig. number 45. This is a carbine with nickel steel barrel, which has been rebarreled and restocked by Hughel's Gunshop, Monroe, Washington.

CHAPTER 3

Remington

THE REMINGTON Arms Company has the distinction of being the oldest arms manufacturer in this country, still in business, as it dates back to 1816.

In our particular field we join Remington in the year 1870, when the famous number 1 Sporting Rifle was introduced. The action of the number 1 was a modification of the Remington Rider rolling block. At its introduction the rifle was chambered for .22 rim fire, but a few years later (after 1873) the .45-70 was made available with the receiver proportionally enlarged to handle the larger cartridge. Barrel lengths available were octagon 28, 30 and 32 inches long, weighing from 9 to 10½ pounds. Pictured on page 48, Fig. 46, is a number 1 rifle, serial number 11037 with a 28 inch octagon barrel.

The Mid-Range Rifle number 1, cal. .40-70, necked, came into being about 1875. Soon after its release it was also made in .45-70 as well as .44-77 necked and .50-70 government. This model was available in the following grades:

A. Sporting stock, combination peep and open rear, Beach front sight, 28 and 30 inch barrels.

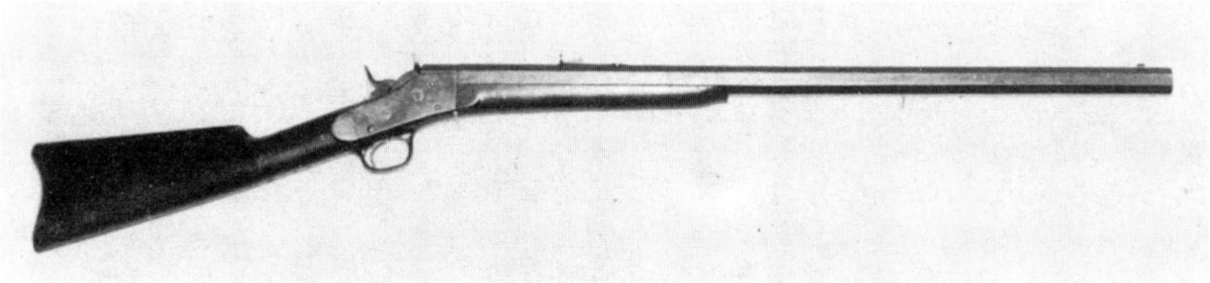

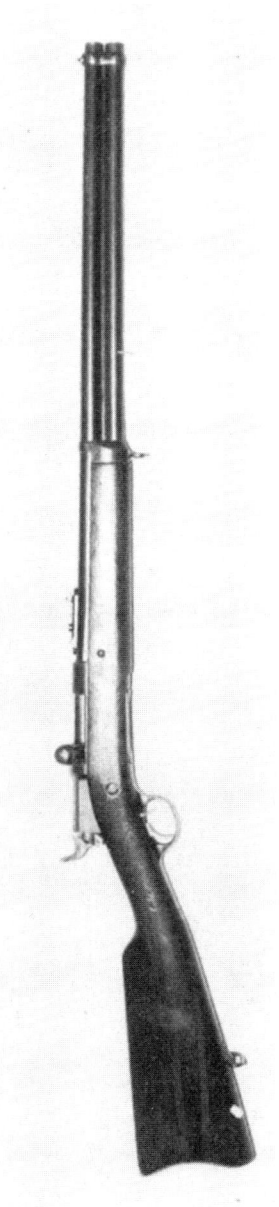

FIG. 46. Number 1 Remington Sporting rifle, serial number 11037. This is the rolling block action. *Author's Collection*

FIG. 47. A plain Remington Keene Sporting rifle. *Author's Collection*

B. Sporting stock, tang peep rear, Beach front sight.

C. Creedmoor stock, pistol grip, tang peep rear, breech front sights.

D. Sporting stock, pistol grip, tang peep rear, wind gauge front sight.

E. Sporting stock, pistol grip, Vernier rear, wind gauge front sight.

F. Creedmoor stock, pistol grip, Vernier rear, wind gauge front sight, rubber butt and tip, and checkered fore-end.

The Black Hills rifle seems to be the same as the number 1 sporting rifle, except that it had a 28 inch round barrel. The Remington catalog describes it as being .45-60 caliber, but this has been proven wrong, as specimens found have all been .45-70.

Both Sharpe and Satterlee list an "Improved" New York State model in our caliber. That would be almost the same as the one adopted by that state in 1871, in the .50-70 caliber, but it is doubtful if this was used by New York.

The Remington Keene rifle is always an arm that will arouse interest in any gun bug. The Keene, patented in 1874 and brought out by Remington in 1880, was of the bolt action variety, with a tubular magazine under the barrel. One of its peculiarities was an exposed hammer on the rear of the bolt. When the bolt was actuated, the hammer came to half-cock and had to be pulled to full-cock manually. Inside the bolt there is a small piece that can be removed so the hammer will come to full-cock when the bolt is closed. It seems that this may have been done on many of these guns, as two of the three in the author's collection are this way. The Keene has a magazine cut-off on the left side of

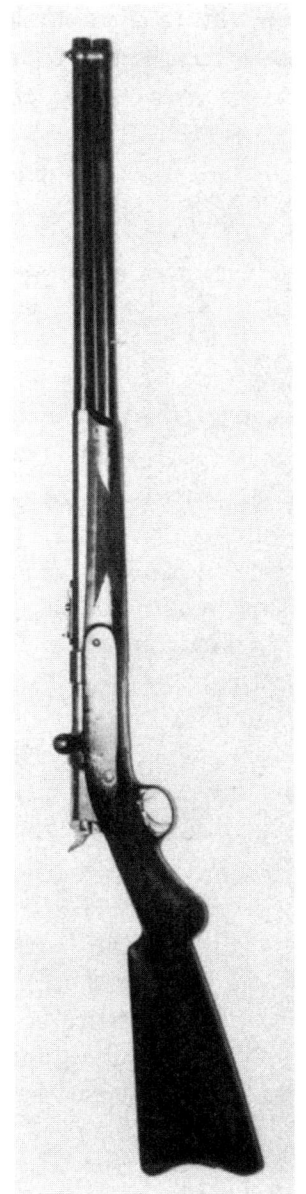

FIG. 48. A fancy grade Remington Keene Sporting rifle, serial number 389.

Author's Collection

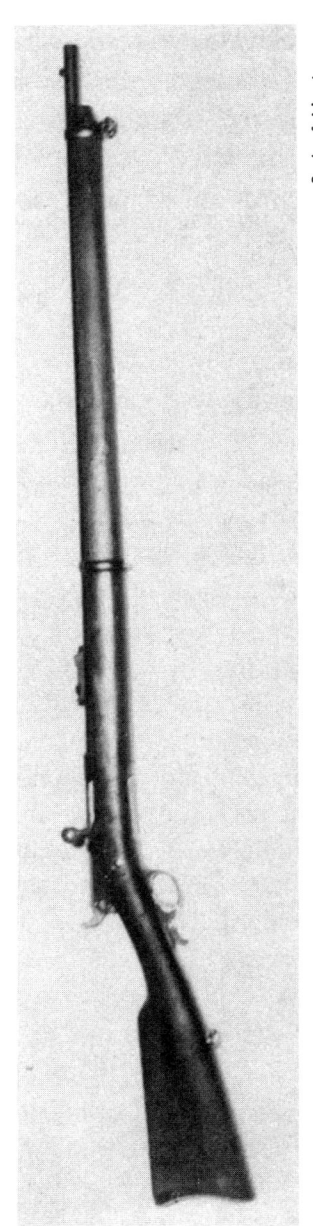

FIG. 49. The Remington Keene Military rifle.

Springfield Armory

the receiver. If a reader should ever wish to disassemble one of these rifles, there is a large screw in the right side of the stock below the receiver that has a left hand thread.

Records show the Keene, Fig. 47, was produced in a standard sporting model with a 24 inch round barrel and full magazine.

In the military field, the navy bought 250 Keene rifles in 1880. This model had a 30 inch barrel, full stock and 9 shot magazines. Shown in Fig. 49 is a Keene military rifle that is on display in the Springfield Armory Museum. A military carbine with 20½ inch barrel was also produced. One of these, serial number 2393 is shown in Fig. 50.

The number 3 Remington Hepburn sporting rifle was especially designed for long range hunting and target purposes requiring the use of heavy charges. It had a solid breech-block with direct rear support, convenient side lever action and rebounding hammer, so that the arm always stood with the trigger in the safety notch, rendering premature discharge impossible. It was chambered for almost all standard black powder cartridges. As standard it could be furnished with half-octagon or full-octagon barrel, oiled walnut stock, pistol grip, checkered, case-hardened frame and mountings, knife blade front and buckhorn rear sights. A typical Hepburn serial number 4402 is shown in Fig. 51.

Although this chapter deals with Remington, it seems fitting that the Lee repeating rifle should be discussed here. The Lee U.S. Navy rifle Model 1879 was a development of the same James P. Lee mentioned in the

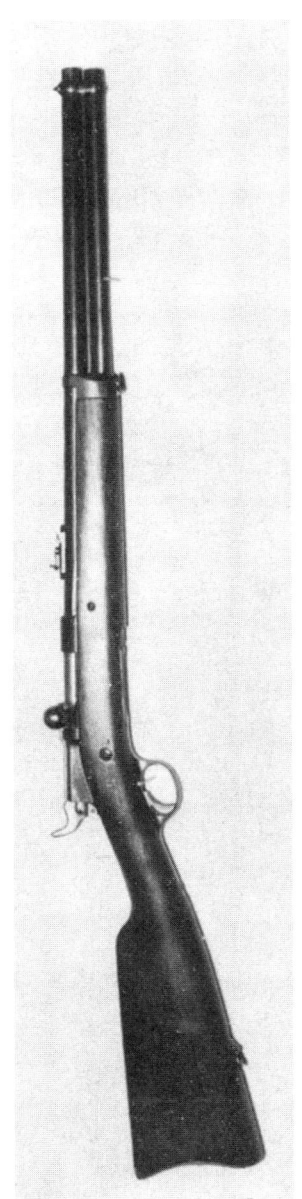

FIG. 50. The Remington Keene Military carbine, serial number 2393.

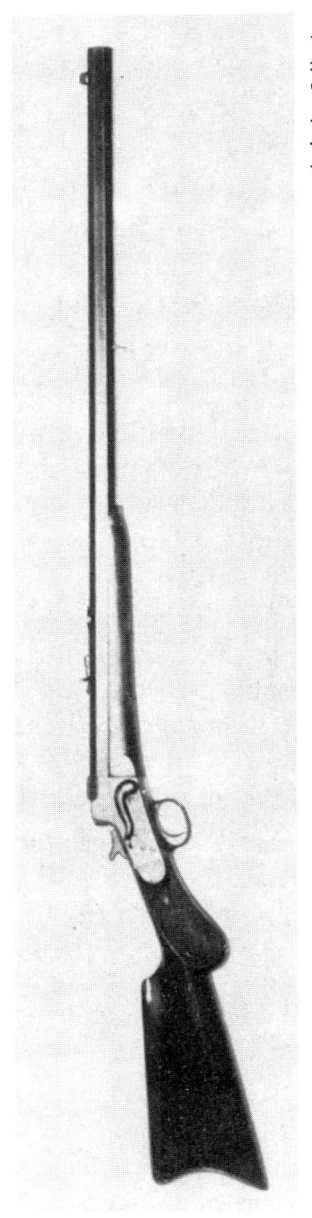

FIG. 51. Number 3 Remington Hepburn, serial number 4402.

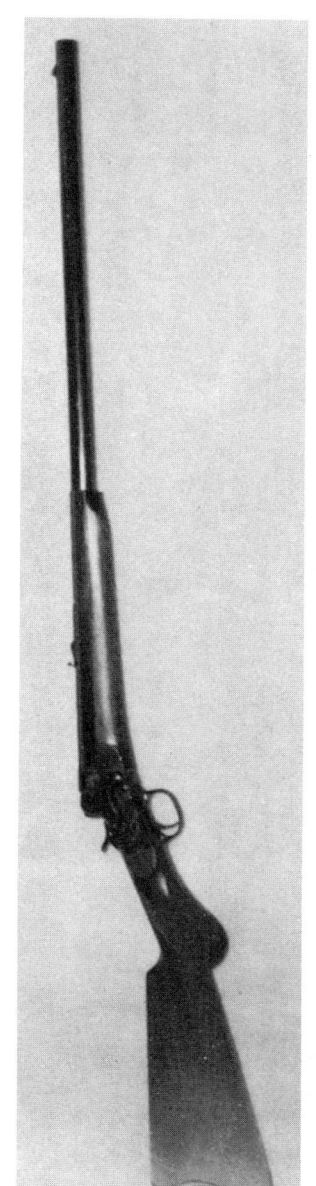

George Rowbottom Collection

FIG. 52. A number 3 Remington Hepburn, serial number 1071, which was in Eliphet Remington's personal collection.

Author's Collection

FIG. 53. The Lee repeating Military rifle, serial number 480.

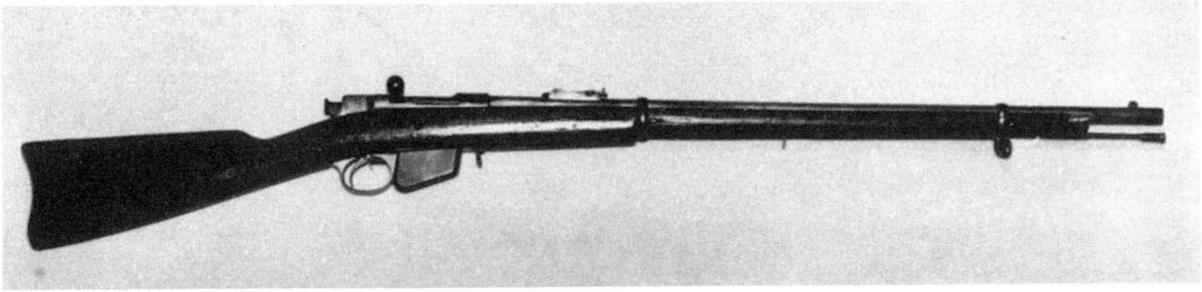

Fig. 54. The Lee repeating Military rifle, serial number 888.

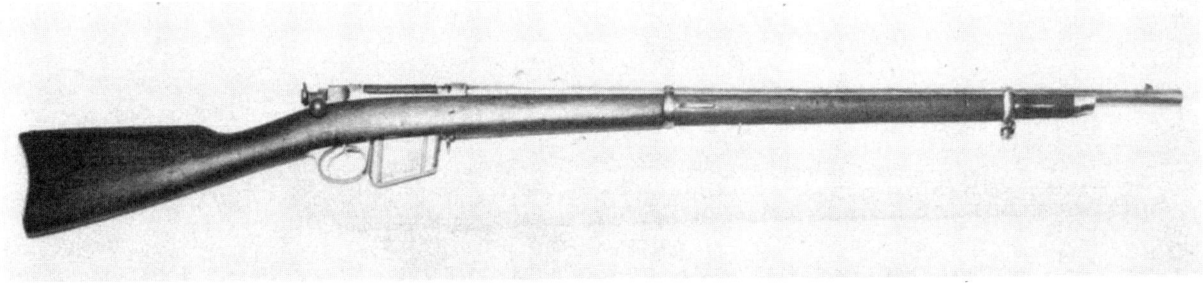

Author's Collection

Fig. 55. A Remington Lee repeating Military rifle, serial number 51058.

Author's Collection

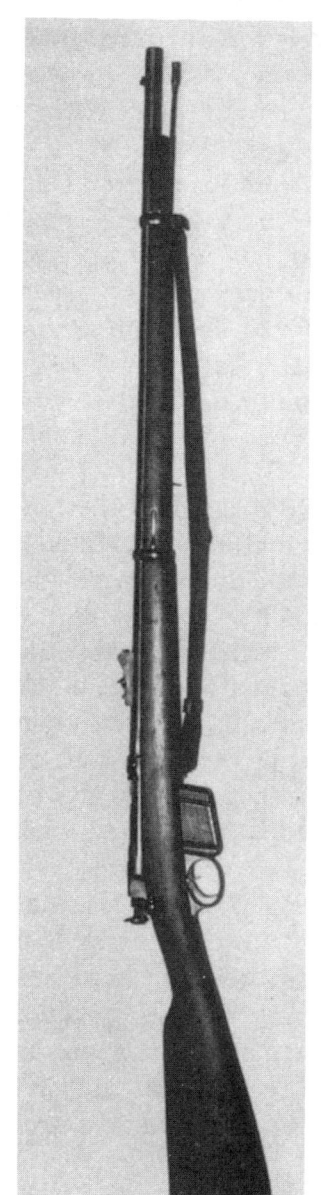

Fig. 56. A Remington Lee repeating Military rifle, serial number 51918.

Author's Collection

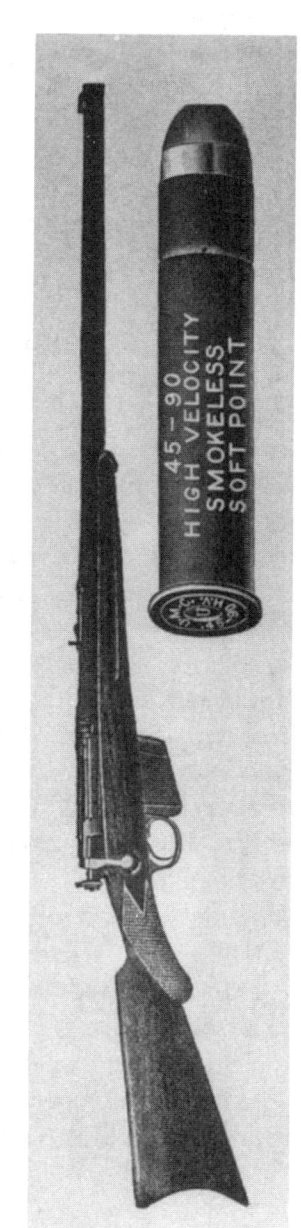

Fig. 57. Typical Remington Lee Sporting rifle.

M. Hartley & Co. Catalog, 1903

chapter on the Springfield. Lee rifles were marked "Lee Arms Co., Bridgeport, Conn." and their mailing address was the same as the Sharps Rifle Co. It is evident that these Lee rifles were made under contract by Sharps. To further substantiate this the writer has a letter (see page 138) in his file. The Lee was a bolt action repeater with a detachable box magazine holding five cartridges. The magazine, located directly forward of the trigger guard, could be immediately removed by depressing a catch in front of the trigger. Barrel length was 28½ inches and overall length about 48 inches. Pictured here are two Lee rifles, Fig. 53 bears serial number 480 and Fig. 54 serial number 888.

In about the year 1880 Remington acquired the Lee patents and introduced the Remington Lee Military rifle of which the navy bought 300 for experimental purposes. This model was essentially the same as the Lee except that the barrel was 32 inches long and the bolt handle was bent down along the side of the stock as on the 1903 Springfield. On pages 54, 55 are shown two Remington-Lee's, both bearing U.S.N. and an anchor over initials W.W.K. on the forward top of the receiver. Fig. 55 is serial number 51058 and Fig. 56, serial number 51918.

A sporting version of the Remington Lee was announced in 1886. It had a 26 inch round barrel, half pistol grip, checkered, rifle butt-plate, case hardened and buckhorn sights. The weight was 8½ pounds. The typical Remington-Lee sporting rifle pictured in Fig. 57, was taken from the 1903, M. Hartley & Company catalog. This was Remington's final rifle in .45-70.

CHAPTER 4

Bullard

THE BULLARD Rifle Co., Springfield, Massachusetts, produced one of the finest lever action repeaters ever made. Mr. Bullard who was for five years, master mechanic at Smith & Wesson developed a rifle whose action was positive and not dependent on springs. In general outside appearance, it was similar to the '86 Winchester, but the action was entirely different. This was self-cocking with a solid breech-block behind the bolt which had to be in place and securely locked in its position for the hammer to reach the firing pin. The bolt was operated by a rack and pinion—the pinion being on the end of the trigger guard lever.

Pictured in Fig. 58, page 58, is a fancy grade Bullard Sporting rifle serial number 571. This specimen has a 28 inch half-octagon barrel, half-magazine and weighs 10 pounds. Fig. 59 is a standard sporting model serial number 932. This one has a half-octagon barrel, full magazine, and weights slightly over 10 pounds.

The following excerpts from the "Bullard Repeating

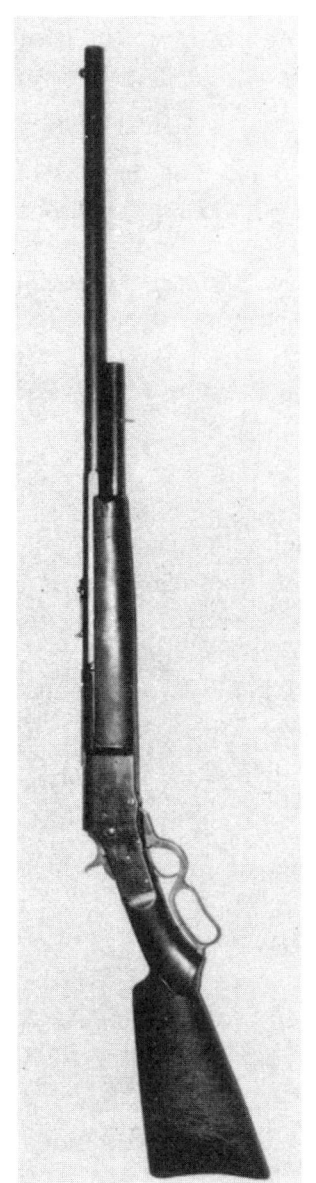

FIG. 58. A better grade Bullard repeating rifle, serial number 571.

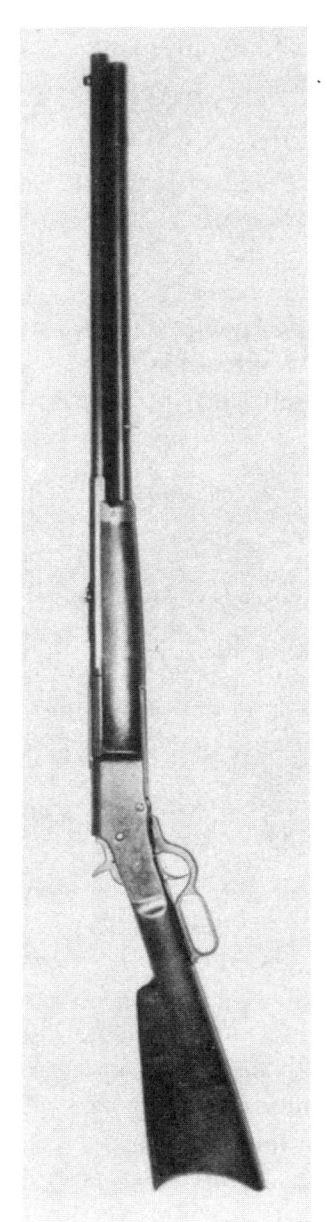

FIG. 59. A standard grade Bullard repeating rifle, serial number 932.

Arms Co." circular give us the full advantage of their repeater:

1st, Safety

The action is positive in all its parts, not dependent on springs. It is self-locking, with a solid breech-block behind the bolt, which must be in place and securely locked, before it is possible for the hammer to reach the firing pin. Before placing this rifle on the market, it was subjected to the most thorough tests as to its strength and endurance, and has stood the heaviest charges without the least sign of weakness.

2nd, Rapidity

It is possible to fire the Bullard with greater rapidity than any other repeating rifle, as it works easier and smoother; for its more direct leverage on the work to be done, the heaviest work being done with the best leverage, as in extracting the cartridge which is started when the lever is in position to exert the greatest strain. The hammer is brought to full cock by direct leverage inside the frame, instead of a sliding motion of bolt or firing-pin, on and over the top on the hammer, which is very often liable to grind and always makes the arm work hard and unpleasant. The Bullard has been fired twelve shots in five seconds, the best record of any other gun being eleven shots in seven seconds, using U.S. cartridges.

3rd, Loading

The magazine is charged from the underside, and it can be done with equal facility by a right or left handed person and as there are no holes or spring covers on the side, it is not possible to have it clogged by passing

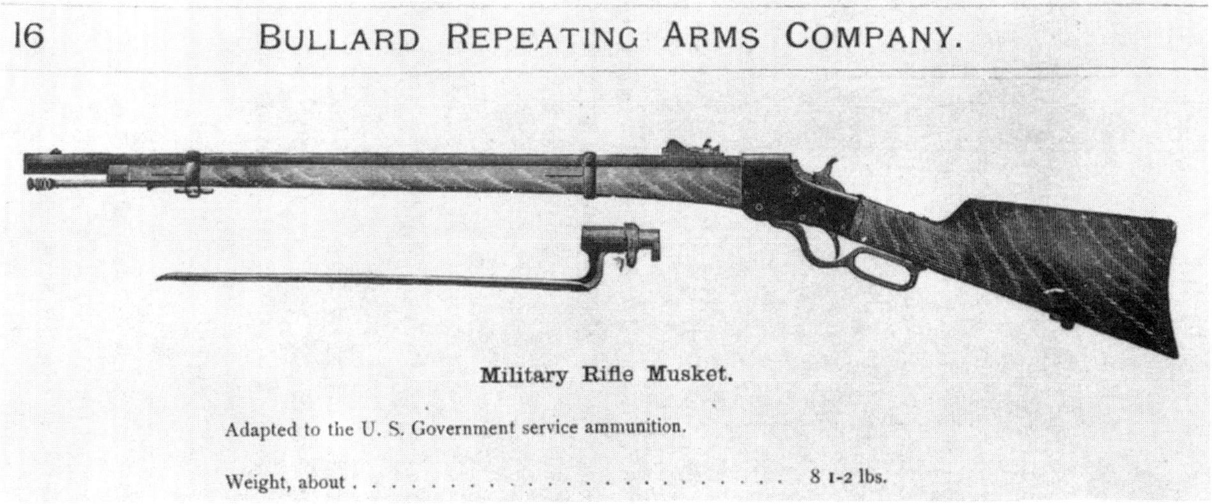

Bullard Company Catalog

FIG. 60. The Bullard Single Shot Military rifle musket.

through brush or laying it on the ground or in trenches, etc. It is much easier to load on horseback than any other gun, as there is more choice of position than when the opening is on the side. It can be loaded as a single loader, either top or bottom, leaving the magazine full at all times for an emergency.

4th

The Bullard is the only lever repeater that will successfully use the regular United States copper cartridge (.45 cal. 70 grs. powder) owing to its absolute certainty to extract the shell, which being made of copper and a folded head, does not contract after firing (as in the case of brass shells) but often sticks in the chamber, a difficulty more frequently mentioned in reports of trials of breech-loading fire arms by Government experts, than any other. The Bullard never fails.

Bullard also shows in the circular a military magazine musket and a military magazine carbine. According to this circular, the musket had a 28 inch round barrel and weighed 10½ pounds and the carbine a 22½ inch barrel and weighed 9½ pounds. The circular also states that this is adapted to U.S. .45-70-405 cartridge. It is believed that very few of the military repeating rifles and carbines were made except on an experimental basis.

The Bullard catalog also shows their famous single shot rifle which has an outward appearance similar to that of the Stevens. The single shot was a very popular and highly praised target rifle made in many other calibers besides .45-70.

The catalog pictures the single shot also as a military musket Fig. 60, and the military single shot carbine. The musket, having a 32 inch round barrel, weighed

8½ pounds while the carbine, a 26 inch round barrel, weighed 8 pounds, and it states that the same breechblock, guard lever, hammer and trigger were used in the repeater.

The circular shows these military single shots being made, although the writer has never seen nor heard of one elsewhere.

CHAPTER 5

Colt

IN A STORY concerning firearms of almost any type, sooner or later appears the name of "Colt." Sam Colt's genius took him into almost all fields of ordnance including the .45-70 rifle. Of all rifles described here, probably the rarest is the double barreled rifle made by Colt. Mr. Fred P. L. Mills of Deerfield, Massachusetts, has recently published a book entitled *Colts Double Rifles*. In this book Mr. Mills goes into detail describing the "Colt Double." From the little information available, it seems that less than 40 were made. There are 13 authentic specimens known. According to Mr. Mills, eight of these are .45-70, one .45-85, one .45-100 and three are unidentified as to caliber.

As most of these seemed to be built as custom guns, barrel lengths vary and naturally weights also. The barrels are from 25 to 28¼ inches. All but one of them has right hand twist in one barrel and left hand twist in the other. Only number 307 owned by Merrill P. Deer of Bergersville, Indiana, pictured here in Fig. 61 has right hand twist in both barrels.

At this point we will depart from .45-70 to .45-85-285 Colt, Marlin & Bullard cartridge. In 1888, Colt

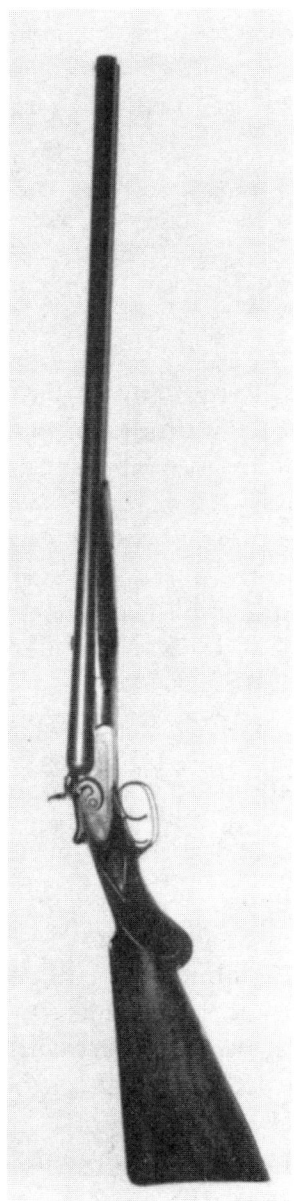

*Courtesy of Merrill P. Deer, and Harry Plummer
Photo by Robert Brant*

FIG. 61. The rare Colt double rifle. Serial number 307.

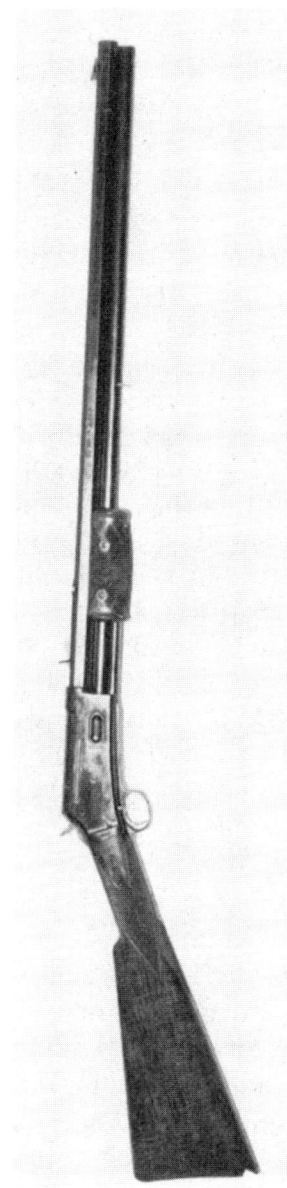

Author's Collection

FIG. 62. A Colt Lightning Express rifle, caliber 45-85-285.

introduced the "New Lightning Magazine Centerfire Rifle," with a long action. This gun had been made since 1885 with a short action that handled the .32-20, .38-40 and .44-40.

The New Express Model, as it was also called, had a longer frame that would handle the .45-85 as well as other similar cartridges. The .45-85-285 was the same case as the .45-70, but used 15 grains more powder and a lighter bullet. The .45-85 Colt, Marlin and Bullard is not to be confused with the .45-85 Winchester which had a case the same length as the .45-90. The Colt Lighting Express rifle was a slide action rifle that enabled the shooter to use heavy cartridges such as those carried by the 1886 Winchester and the 1881 Marlin with much greater rapidity than with the lever action. This Colt rifle was made in 3 basic sizes. The rifle which is pictured in Fig. 62, page 64, has a 28 inch octagon barrel.

The weight was approximately 10 pounds and a round barrel 9¾ pounds. This was also furnished in a carbine model with 22 inch round barrel and 8 shot capacity at about 9 pounds and also in a baby carbine with the same dimensions as the carbine, but with the weight trimmed to approximately 8 pounds. The action on this gun was unique in that the hammer was locked back until the cartridge entered the chamber and the bolt was locked. This eliminated the possibility of firing with the breech partially open. Also, the action had to be completely locked before a second cartridge was fed from the magazine into the carrier. The gun loaded in the conventional method—through the loading gage on the side of the receiver, but it could only be loaded

Author's Collection

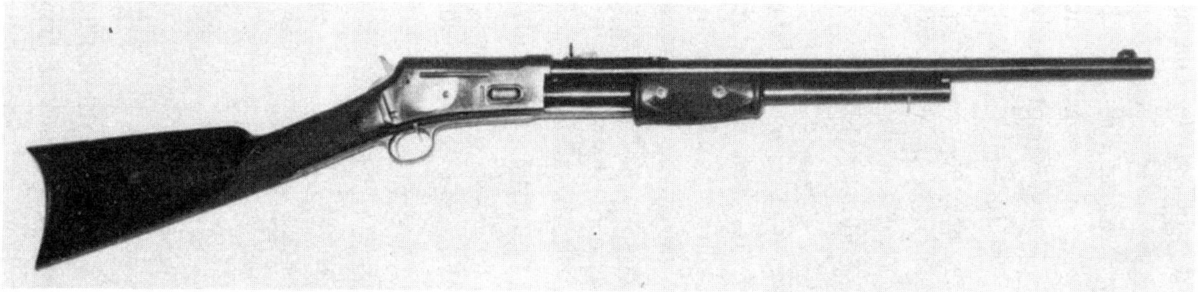

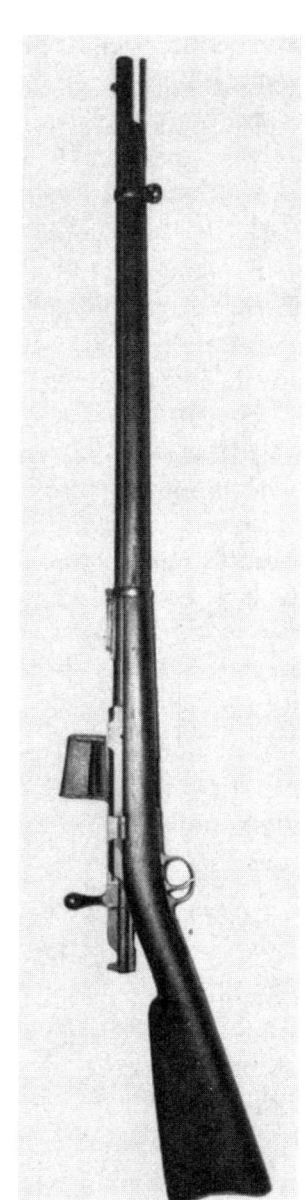

Fig. 63. The author's favorite hunting rifle. A rebarreled Colt Lightning express rifle.

Colt Museum

Fig. 64. General Franklin's experimental rifle made by Colt.

with the action open. The standard type tubular magazine was used.

Another feature of the Lightning Express Rifle which enabled the shooter to fire quickly, was that if the trigger was held depressed and the action continuously operated, the moment the action was locked the hammer was released, thus firing the cartridge without having to release and again pull the trigger. This feature was not accepted in some circles as it was thought it was not entirely safe from accidental discharge after firing the first shot.

As a personal note injected here, Fig. 63 shows one of the above mentioned rifles that has been rebarreled by the author using a Gattling machine gun barrel cut to 22 inches and turned as light as possible. This piece is naturally chambered for .45-70. The original barrel was .38-56. Some slight alterations in the carriers were needed to make this change. This rifle has shown good hunting accuracy and found to be very deadly on whitetail deer for brush shooting in Maine.

A little known repeating rifle made by Colt, probably in a quantity totaling no more than 50, was the Franklin magazine gun. This was invented by Gen. W. B. Franklin a veteran of the Civil War and later a Vice President of Colt, and was patented on February 2, 1875. The action on this gun was of the bolt type. The Franklin had a barrel length of $32\frac{1}{2}$ inches and also had a full military type stock. It is also noted that the famous Buffington rear sight was used on the Franklin repeating rifle.

A peculiar feature of the Franklin, an example of which is shown in Fig. 64, is that a detachable box magazine was mounted above the barrel. The cartridges in this magazine were fed by gravity when the bolt was pulled toward the rear. Also the fired cartridge after extraction was ejected only by gravity through the bottom of the receiver to the ground.

An earlier version of the Franklin was said to have a tubular magazine above the barrel.

Later, in the chapter on automatic weapons, the Colt "Gattling" gun will be described.

CHAPTER 6

Sharps

NO BOOK covering early American cartridge rifles would be complete without mentioning the story of Christian Sharps. Sharps had to his credit ten different patents, the most famous of which covered the breech loading rifle patent number 5763, issued September 12, 1848. It was from this basic design that the later Sharps cartridge rifles were developed.

During the life of the Sharps rifle, the Sharps Co. had five different locations and several different names. Our interest in the story begins in 1874 when the firm was reorganized as the Sharps Rifle Co. and operated in Hartford, Connecticut. In 1876 the company again moved to Bridgeport and operations continued until 1881 when the company was dissolved.

The Sharps rifle won its great fame in the Civil War, as the government bought many thousands of the .52 caliber carbines using linen cartridges. The accuracy of these rifles in the hands of Union mounted infantry is where the term "Sharpshooter" originated. After the war many of these percussion breech loading Sharps were altered to both .50-70 and .45-70 caliber. The one shown in Fig. 65, page 70, is such a specimen.

The one pictured there still has the original lock with

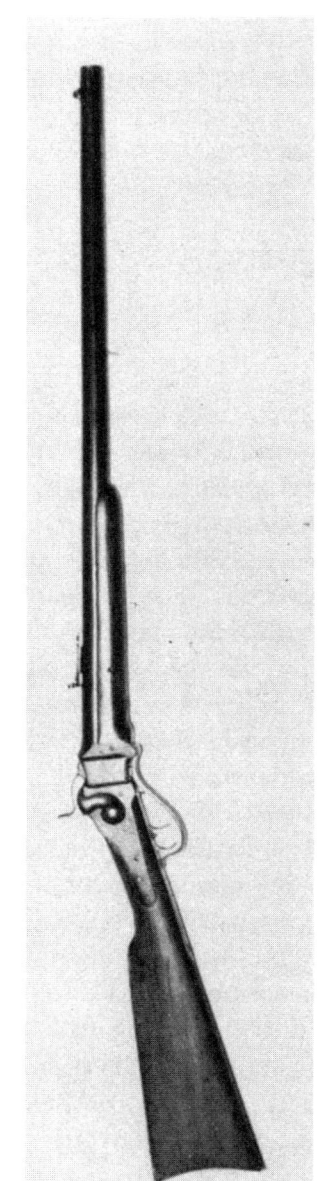

Fig. 65. A Sharp's percussion carbine converted to .45-70. Serial number 98813.

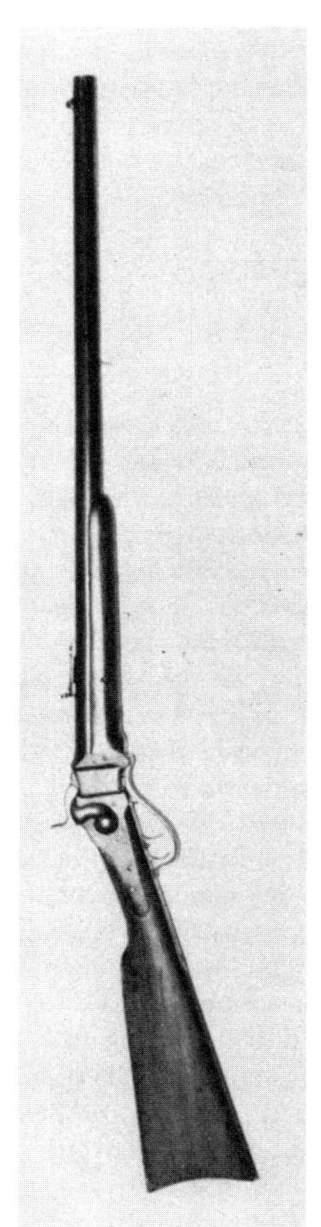

Fig. 66. The Sharp's "Business 45."

the Lawrence pellet priming device, and has been rebarreled at the factory to .45 caliber and had the action altered to take the extractor for the brass cases. It also has a new breech-block to accommodate the firing pin and the percussion hammer has been replaced.

Model 1874 was the first Sharps rifle completely designed for metallic cartridges and the .45-70 cartridge. Sharps catalog of 1878 speaks of the .45 caliber as follows:

"Rifles of .45 caliber having proved to give much better results and greater satisfaction to our customers, we have discontinued the manufacture of either the .44 or .50 caliber except on special orders. The .45 caliber Sporting and Business rifles chambered for the 2 1/10 (.45-70) or 2 ⅞ inch shell will be found entirely effective and in every way satisfactory for either medium or heavy charges of powder. All of our rifles are warranted to stand 150 grains of powder if customer desires to use that quantity, but the regular charge is ample for any purpose. For long distances any powder that is not burned in the barrel impairs accuracy to such an extent that all benefits from the increase of force is lost, and for short or medium distances the force supplied by the regular charge is sufficient for all requirements."

In this catalog, they list Sharps sporting rifle model 1874 caliber .45, 30 inch octagon barrel, weight 9 to 12 pounds, open sights polished stock and single trigger at a price of $38.00. Also listed and pictured in Fig. 66 is the Sharps business rifle model 1874 with 28 inch round barrel .40 and .45 calibers (specimen shown is .45-70) double triggers, polished stock, weight about 10½ pounds at a price of $35.00.

Author's Collection

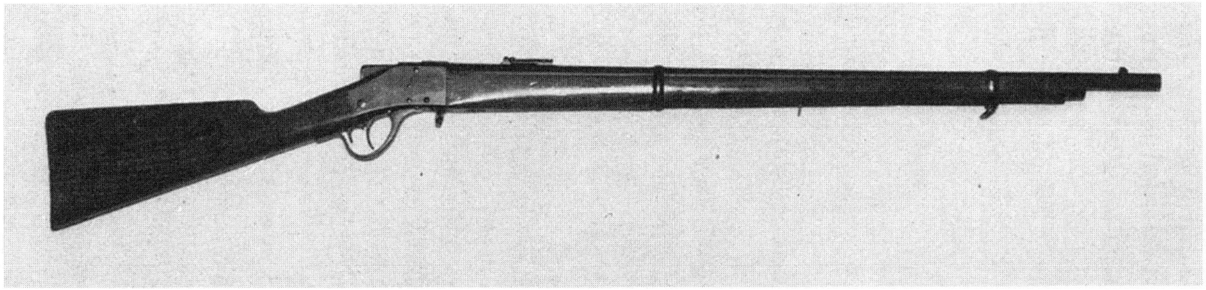

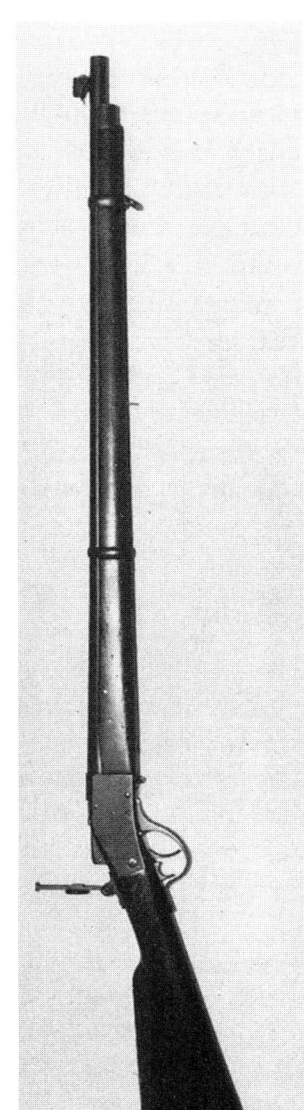

Fig. 67. The Sharp's Bouchardt Military musket.

Author's Collection

Fig. 68. The Sharp's Bouchardt Military musket.

In 1878 Sharps procured the Bouchardt patent. The rifles made and known as the Sharps-Bouchardt are one of the most beautiful and highly prized single shot rifles of the black powder era.

The best explanation of this action and of the military rifle and carbine made on it is from the 1878 catalog as follows:

"For safety, accuracy, penetration, range, ease of manipulation rapidity and certainty of fire, strength, durability, and lightness of recoil, they are unequaled by any rifle made.

These are built in .45 caliber, with length of shell 2-1/10 inches, 75 grains powder, 420 grains lead, U.S. cartridges can be used, length of barrel 32 inches, length of rifle 48½ inches, weight without bayonet 9 pounds.

        Price without bayonet $20.00
        Price with bayonet   22.50

For government, states, and independent military organizations special prices will be given upon application. The operation of this rifle is remarkable for its simplicity and ease of manipulation. Throwing down the lever (which serves also for a trigger guard) ejects with certainty the exploded shell, and cocks the rifle; the same motion also automatically moves the safety-catch and locks the trigger so that accidental discharge is impossible.

The cartridge is now inserted and the lever returned to its position. The rifle, though now at full cock, may be carried and handled in any manner with perfect safety, there is nothing to catch in bushes, it may be pulled out of a boat or wagon by the muzzle, or handled in any manner, however carelessly (for other rifles),

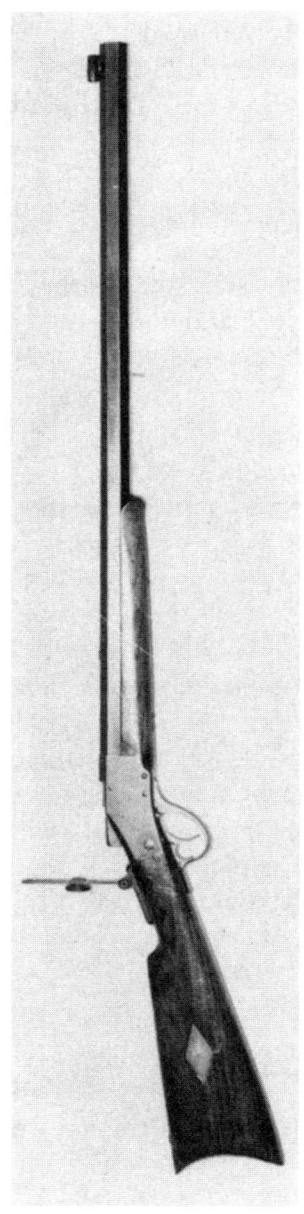

FIG. 69. A Sharp's Bouchardt Sporting rifle with 30 inch heavy octagonal barrel.

Author's Collection

and it cannot be discharged, except by intentionally releasing the safety-catch and pulling the trigger. The safety-catch is so located behind the trigger, and under the trigger-guard, that it can be instantaneously, but in no case accidentally released.

When great rapidity of fire is desirable, as in battles, the safety lever, may be quickly removed so that the piece can be discharged immediately upon closing the breech, and thus save one movement. The United States and Austrian nations are now the only great Governments who retain the obsolete outside hammer on their arms, and the questions of a change is being agitated by the latter. Objections may possibly be made to the absence of the outside hammer on account of the difficulty in executing the movement of support and not arms. It should be remembered that the manual is made for arms, and not arms for the manual. It is vastly more important, when an enemy is approaching, to be able to shoot him effectually, than to salute him gracefully.

Pictured in Figs. 67 and 68 are two of the military Bouchardt rifles in the author's collection. Also pictured in Fig. 69 is a Sharps Bouchardt sporting rifle with a 30 inch heavy octagon barrel weighing about 12 pounds.

Referring again to the military Bouchardt, Sharps also made a carbine with a 24 inch barrel weighing $7\frac{1}{2}$ pounds that sold for $18.50. Double set triggers could be had on either rifle or carbine for $4.00 extra.

Also listed in the 1879 catalog was the officer's rifle described as "Same length, weight and caliber as the military rifle, medium fancy American walnut stock, closely selected barrels, with receiver inlaid with hard rubber (similar to Long Range Rifle) extra finish throughout. Price $30.00."

CHAPTER 7

Marlin & Ballard

WE WILL CONSIDER the Ballard and Marlin rifles together as our interest in the Ballard rifle begins at the time John Marlin started manufacturing them in 1876. Previously the famous Ballard rifles had been made by Ball & Williams of Worcester, Massachusetts, Merrimak Arms & Mfg. Co., Newburyport, Massachusetts, and the Brown Mfg. Co. Each of these succeeded the other after their failure.

The basic principle of the Ballard rifle was a falling block single shot type action actuated by the conventional under lever that also served as a trigger guard. Its biggest feature was that as the breech block rose it also was cammed forward against the head of the cartridge securely sealing the breech. The model variations of the Ballard were numerous those regularly chambered for the .45-70 are listed below.

The Ballard Hunters Rifle No. 1½ was introduced in 1879. This rifle had a heavy iron frame and was made with a round barrel. The barrel lengths available were 28, 30, and 32 inches. The rifle weighed from 9 to 10½ pounds. When it was first introduced it was made available in a .45-70 caliber. Later it was manufactured in other calibers.

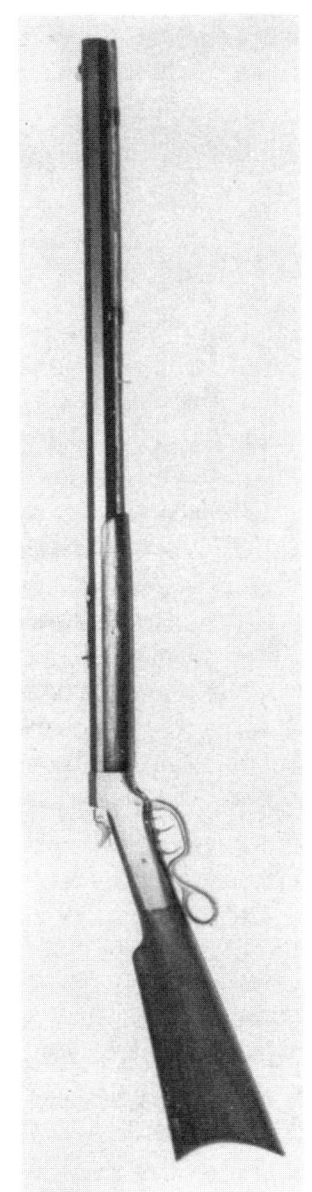

FIG. 70. The number 5 Pacific Ballard, typical style with double set triggers and loop lever. *Author's Collection*

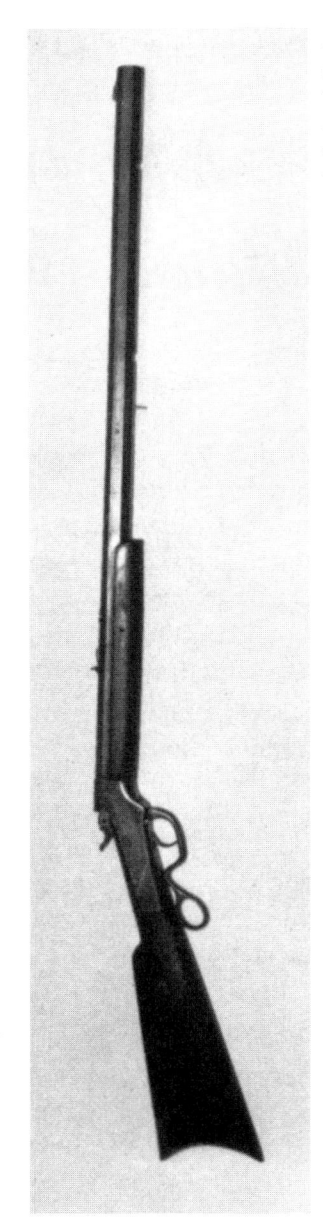

FIG. 71. This rifle is believed to be a number 4¼ Ballard. The cleaning rod is missing. *Author's Collection*

The Ballard Far West No. 1¾ rifle was the same as No. 1½ rifle except for the addition of double set triggers, and was used mostly for target shooting. It was available with the same length barrels as the No. 1½.

Probably the most common of the Ballard rifles in our caliber is the No. 5 which was called the Pacific model. This model was made in a very wide range of calibers and naturally amongst them the .45-70. After all other calibers were discontinued this one was still made. .45-70. It was regularly manufactured with a heavy octagon barrel and double set triggers. The lever was of the small loop style. A feature which makes the Pacific easy to recognize is that under the barrel a wooden cleaning rod was carried. The Pacific rifle shown here Fig. No. 70 bears serial number 25458.

Another model that was very similar to the Pacific was the No. 4¼ Ballard. About the only major difference between the 4¼ and the No. 5 was that the 4¼ did not have double set triggers. Fig. 71 shows what the author believes to be the No. 4¼ Ballard with the exception that the cleaning rod is missing.

The first Marlin repeating rifle was the Model 1881, a lever action repeater made simple and strong. The following is an excerpt from the Marlin catalog dated August 15, 1888.

The Marlin Repeating Rifle Model 1881

The operation of this gun is of the simplest kind, and yet the action is exceedingly strong. By merely operating the lever back and forth, which can be done without removing the rifle from the shoulder, the cartridge just discharged is ejected, a new cartridge carried from the magazine into the chamber, the hammer set at full cock and the gun is again ready to fire. The 28 inch magazine, which is the standard size, holds 9 cartridges and one can be placed in the barrel; all 10 shots can be fired ordinarily in six to seven seconds, and by actual timing this has been done in less than five seconds.

The action of a magazine gun is the part on which the arm depends for the proper performance of its work; this in the Marlin, is of the "Bolt" class.

The bolt comes solidly up to the base of the cartridge, covering it entirely; through this all danger is avoided, though a defective cartridge should happen to be used. A premature explosion positively cannot occur, and the greater the recoil, the more firmly the bolt is held in place. These are a few of the salient points and advantages which this rifle has over others. This powerful action has been produced by careful experiments and trials, and we have succeeded in adjusting the breech mechanism so as to meet every requirement.

The cartridges are loaded into the magazine at the side of the frame and can be inserted either with the lock open or closed. When the bolt is withdrawn, the cartridge at the bottom of the magazine enters the carrier block gradually, avoiding concussion produced in some other makes of magazine guns, by the sudden jump of the whole column of cartridges, with a momentum, in some cases, sufficient to explode a sensitive primer.

All the advantages of a single breech loader are also contained in the Marlin; it can be used with great rapidity, the cartridge being inserted into the barrel instead of the magazine, and cartridges specially loaded with patched bullets into the magazine as the patches are liable to become torn in so doing.

We have added one very valuable feature to this rifle, which every sportsman will appreciate. It is an arrangement to prevent clogging of the mechanism when cartridges are used which are shorter than regular, either loaded so, to reduce the charge, or in which the bullets have settled down through continued jolting in the magazine. With this improvement, it is immaterial whether the cartridges used are of regular length or shorter; they are certain to work through the magazine without a hitch. Rifles not having such a provision are very liable to become entirely useless, sometimes at the most inopportune, and perhaps dangerous moment, because all cartridges, unless loaded with extreme care, are more or less liable to permit the bullet to force into the shell beyond the crimping point.

This same improvement must not be understood as permitting any cartridge of the same caliber to be used in these rifles, but only the regular size of shell for which the rifle may be chambered. The charge of powder and lead, however, can be adjusted in any desirable manner, and reduced as much as may be wanted.

The model 1881, in the caliber under discussion, was furnished in the following sizes and weights: .45 caliber, 70 grains powder, 405 grains lead (or 85 grains powder, 285 grains lead)

24 in. Octagon barrel	8 shots— 9 pounds	shotgun butt	$21.00
28 in. Octagon barrel	10 shots— 9½ pounds	shotgun butt	22.50
30 in. Octagon barrel	10 shots—11 pounds	shotgun butt	25.00

Also a lighter model in this caliber made especially for the export trade designated .45-70 "light" as follows:

24 in. Octagon barrel	8 shots 8¼ pounds	shotgun butt	$21.00
28 in. Octagon barrel	10 shots 8¾ pounds	shotgun butt	22.50

Author's Collection

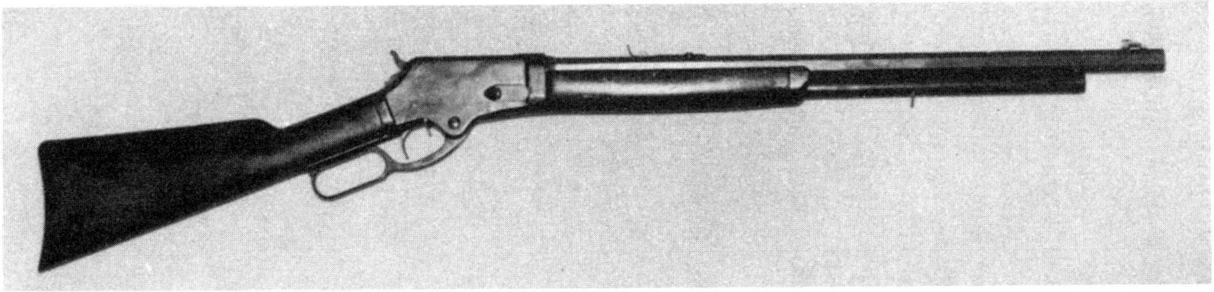

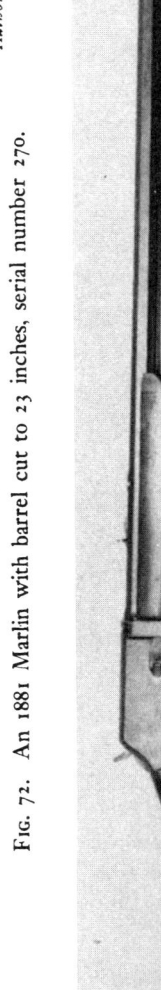

Fig. 72. An 1881 Marlin with barrel cut to 23 inches, serial number 270.

Author's Collection

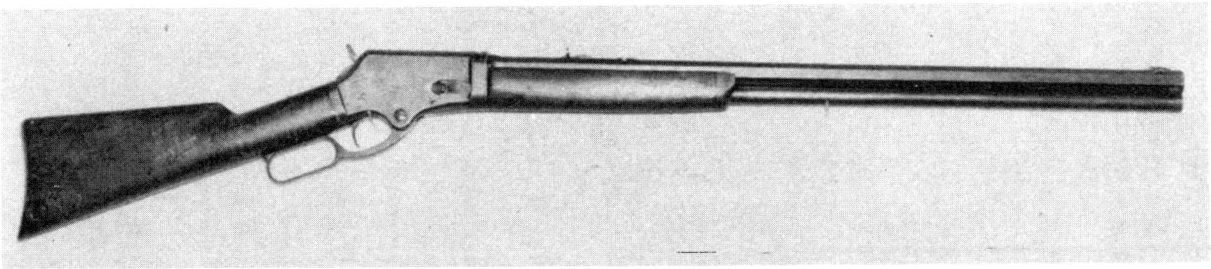

Fig. 73. Another 1881 Marlin with 26 inch full octagon barrel, serial number 2976.

Double set triggers for the above $4.00 extra.

(Note—Here again we see .45-70 and .45-85 used interchangeably)

Pictured in Figs. 72 and 73 are Model 1881 Marlin serial number 270, 23 inch Octagon barrel and 2/3 magazine (this I believe has been cut off) serial number 2976 —28 inches octagon barrel and full magazine, and Fig. 74 serial number 5017 with 28 inch barrel also and number 1 engraving, grade B checkering, and double set triggers. This specimen was shipped from Marlin July 5, 1883. (Their records do not go lower than serial number 4,000).

Marlin Model 1895

Marlin's final rifle in our caliber was the model 1895. This was a beefed up version of the models 1893 and 1894, beefed up and lengthened to take the long and larger cartridge. The '95 was of the famous Marlin solid top side ejection design, which allows a central, low mounted scope on a lever action rifle, if anyone should want to put a scope on a .45-70 hunting rifle.

Marlin describes the solid top models in their catalog as follows:

Claims of Superiority

Safety—The Marlin solid-top receiver insured increased safety to the user. In all of our arms, the top of the action, which is the portion coming between the cartridge and the shooter's head, is not cut into in any way, but is left as a solid shield, making an accident to the shooter almost impossible. There is at all times a solid wall of metal between your head and the cartridge.

In using the old style system, opening on top, there is a chance of accident and injury, either from defective cartridges giving out around the head, a "hang fire" (the cartridge not exploding immediately on the blow of the firing pin, but a fraction of time later, when perhaps the action is partially opened), or someone of the many unaccountables for which guns and ammunition are proverbially famous. With a solid-top frame there is less liability to accident from any of these causes. Neither can there be a premature discharge in a Marlin. The action is so adjusted that a cartridge cannot be exploded until the action has first been locked.

Convenience—The side-ejecting principle is a great comfort, as well as a safety, for the empty shells are never ejected into your face; they never cross the line of sight; never interfere with the aim for the next shot; and your eyes and lungs are never filled with smoke and gases. The solid-top also makes it impossible for rain, snow, falling leaves and twigs, pine needles, etc., to get into the action, as the top is always closed and consequently the action protected; there are no crevices for rain, etc., to leak through, and there is no hollow-top to catch and hold the rain.

The system can be used as a single shot with the greatest facility. It is only necessary to drop the cartridges into the opening left by the breech bolt when the action is open, and then close the lever.

Bullets will sometimes be jammed down into the shell by continued jolting in transportation, or shells may be reloaded with light bullets to make a short-range cartridge. In either case the Marlin action will accommodate the cartridge perfectly as long as the regular shell is used. The rifle will take anything varying in length from the empty shell as a minimum up to the full-size cartridge as a maximum. In our models 1893, 1894 and 1895, a very effective and extremely simple device is introduced to permit this. A projection on the lower side of the carrier is acted against by the cam on the lever in such a manner that, as the lever is thrown down and a cartridge enters the carrier, the carrier is slightly raised and partially closes the magazine, and no matter how short the first cartridge may be, the head of the following one will strike against the front of the carrier and can not enter it until the lever is again closed. Cartridges loaded with round bullets can therefore be used in these models.

Very often cartridges which are much alike, as for instance .38 and .44 caliber, get mixed. We have found .44 caliber cartridges among the .38s having been so shipped from the factory. In most cases a person using a rifle and getting a larger cartridge into it, is in trouble and cannot get out the cartridge without taking the gun apart. With our rifle if such a cartridge gets into a smaller caliber gun, all you have to do, when you find your lever will not close with a cartridge in the chamber, is to extract and eject the misfit cartridge by throwing forward your lever, exactly as if it were an empty shell.

This is the only repeating rifle on which a telescope can be conveniently used. A telescope can be fitted to our rifle just as to a single shot, for the action in no way interferes with it being placed as far back as is desired. Many people desire repeaters, but also wish to use them with telescopes for fine shooting. To all such we can recommend our repeaters with greatest confidence. We do not fit telescopes at the factory, but any of the telescope makers will do so at moderate charges. We have

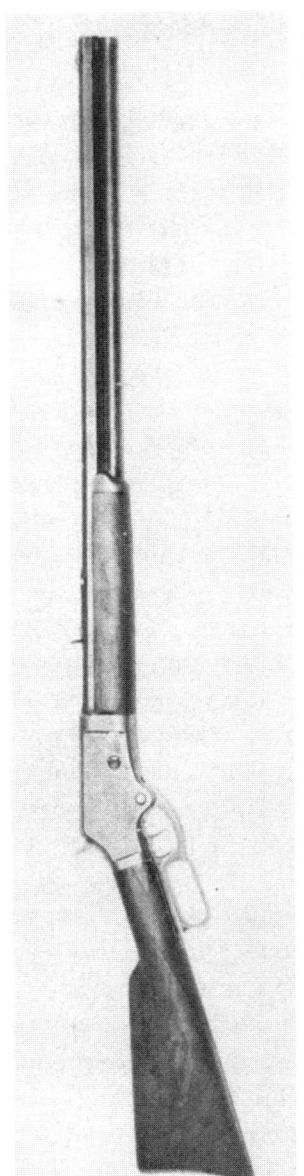

FIG. 74. An engraved and checkered 1881 Marlin, serial number 5017.

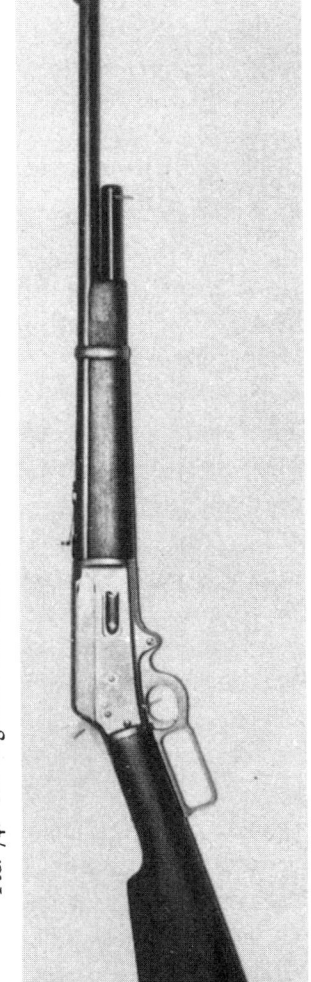

FIG. 75. The side ejection, model 1895, Marlin carbine, serial number 138500.

furnished many rifles to be so fitted, and they have given the greatest satisfaction.

Simplicity—Our repeaters have the fewest parts, and all parts act directly upon each other, without intervening links, connections, etc. In consequence, the action is especially easy in its working, and also simpler in construction. The only tool necessary to remove the working parts of our rifles is one screwdriver, all the essential screws being made with practically the same head.

Accuracy—As the barrels now used in our rifles are the same as the old Ballard barrels in every respect, we regard this as sufficient recommendation of their shooting qualities and durability. The Ballard barrels have always been justly considered, even up to the present day, as the standard of accuracy. Our repeaters will not suffer by comparison.

Our barrels are rifled deeper than other makes. This costs us more money, but we believe it is better so, because deep rifling does not foul as quickly as shallow rifling. Deep rifling puts a greater friction and resistance on the bullet, thereby developing the powder pressure to a higher degree, and getting a more complete combustion. This is one reason why Marlin barrels give better penetration than others when used with exactly the same cartridges. Deep rifling will out-wear and out-last shallow rifling. We also cut our rifling slowly, taking the lightest possible chip at each stroke of the cutter. This, also, costs us more; but in this way we get the smoothest and most perfect rifling and the smallest possible burr on the corners of the lands. After rifling we do not have to put our barrels into scouring machines and scour out the inside with coarse emery, but each barrel is finished inside by hand.

We were the first to introduce light-weight repeaters, and in this move have been followed by all other manufacturers. We were the first to make repeating rifles with a solid top receiver and side ejection, and the only firm making a full line with this superior construction.

Manufacture—In Marlin rifles there are no brazed joints, no cast iron, malleable iron, or cheap metal of any kind. Every part is strong, made from solid stock drop forged. As an illustration we show our receiver and trigger plate, which represent perfectly our system of manufacturing all the parts. The receiver, for instance, is drop forged from high grade bar steel, made specially for us for this purpose and comes to the machine a solid metal block.

Variations of the Model '95 were many—

Carbine with 15 inch round barrel 5 shots 7 pounds	$15.00
Carbine with 22 inch round barrel 8 shots 7¾ pounds	15.00
Rifle with 20 inch round barrel 7 shot 8¼ pounds	15.50
Rifle with 26 inch round barrel 9 shot 8¾ pounds	15.50
Rifle with 28 inch round barrel 10 shot 9 pounds	17.00
Rifle with 30 inch round barrel 10 shot 9¼ pounds	18.50
Rifle with 32 inch round barrel 10 shot 9½ pounds	20.00
Rifle with 20 inch octagon barrel 7 shot 8¼ pounds	16.75
Rifle with 26 inch octagon barrel 9 shot 8¾ pounds	16.75
Rifle with 28 inch octagon barrel 10 shot 9 pounds	18.25
Rifle with 30 inch octagon barrel 10 shot 9¼ pounds	19.75
Rifle with 32 inch octagon barrel 10 inch 9½ pounds	21.25

Pictured in Fig. 75 is a model 95 carbine serial number 138500 which left the Marlin firm in 1895.

CHAPTER 8

Peabody &
Peabody Martini

ON JULY 22, 1862, Mr. Henry L. Peabody was issued U.S. Patent number 35,947. The Peabody patent covered a falling breech action that was hinged at the rear end, and operated by a lever that also served as trigger guard. The early Peabody was one of 65 rifles submitted to the Army Board in Springfield in 1865.

These arms were put through a number of severe tests and the number surviving these first tests were only 8. Later, these 8 remaining rifles were then exposed to the elements and permitted to rust for 10 days and were daily soaked with water.

After this they were again left outside in winter weather where snow and ice covered them, and thawed out by being placed in high temperatures without cleaning. This left only 4 of the 8.

These 4 rifles were than fired with ever increasing charges of powder and lead. Only the Peabody could stand a charge of 120 grains of powder and five ounces of lead. But the war was now over and the need for

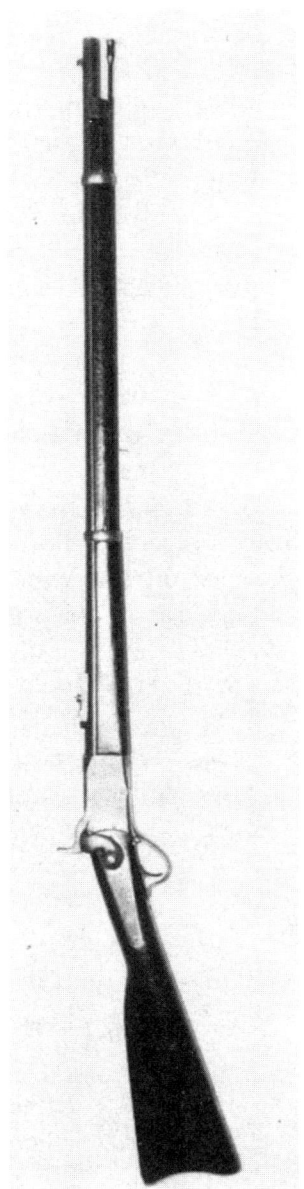

FIG. 76. Peabody Military musket from Connecticut Militia, number 1017. *Author's Collection*

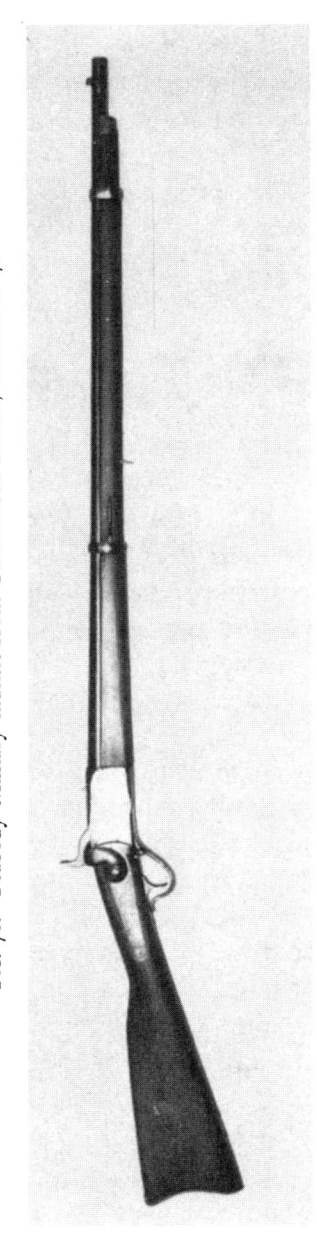

FIG. 77. Peabody Military musket from Connecticut Militia, number 878. *Author's Collection*

arms had ceased, so the findings of the board were tabled for the time being.

According to any records the author can find, the State of Connecticut adopted the Peabody for its guard in a special .433 caliber, but I have in my collection two of these rifles with the Connecticut name plate in the stock that are definitely .45-70 as I cast the chambers and slugged the bore to prove it. This probably means that after the U. S. Government standardized on .45 caliber, Connecticut followed suit.

The two shown, Figs. 76 and 77 are 53 ¾ inches overall with 33 inch barrels and bear serial number Conn. 1017 and serial number Conn. 878 respectively.

The Providence Tool Co. of Providence, Rhode Island manufactured both the Peabody and the Peabody Martini rifles. These two rifles are practically the same. The main difference being that the Martini version was hammerless.

In .45-70, the Peabody-Martini listed the "Kill Deer" and the "Rough & Ready" models. The former had a 28 or 30 inch half-octagon barrel. A specimen seen recently by the author had target sights and was engraved "Kill Deer" on one side of the action. The latter had a 30 inch round barrel.

A Creedmoor grade known as the "What Cheer" was made in .44/95/500 "What Cheer" cartridge. It had a 32 inch half-round barrel and was engraved "Peabody-Martini" on one side of the action and "Creedmoor" on the reverse.

Shown in Fig. 78 is such an action with the above engraving and a 30 inch half-round barrel. It is stamped .45-70 on the top of the barrel and also is stamped A. O. Niedner, Malden, Mass. Mr. Niedner's name also ap-

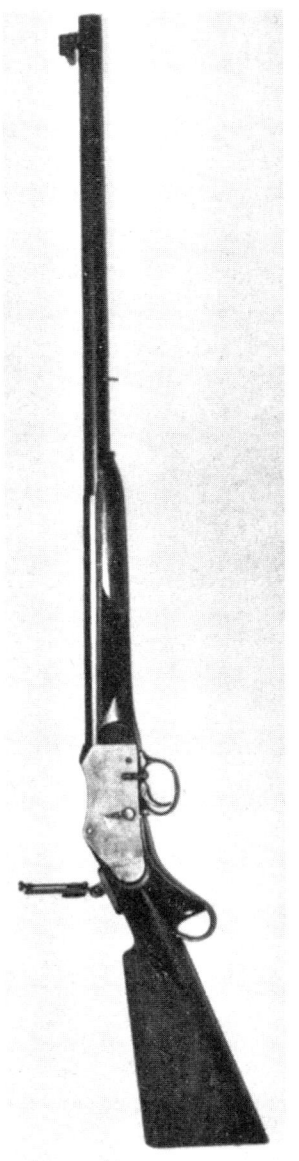

FIG. 78. Peabody-Martin Creedmoor rechambered by A. O. Niedner.

Author's Collection

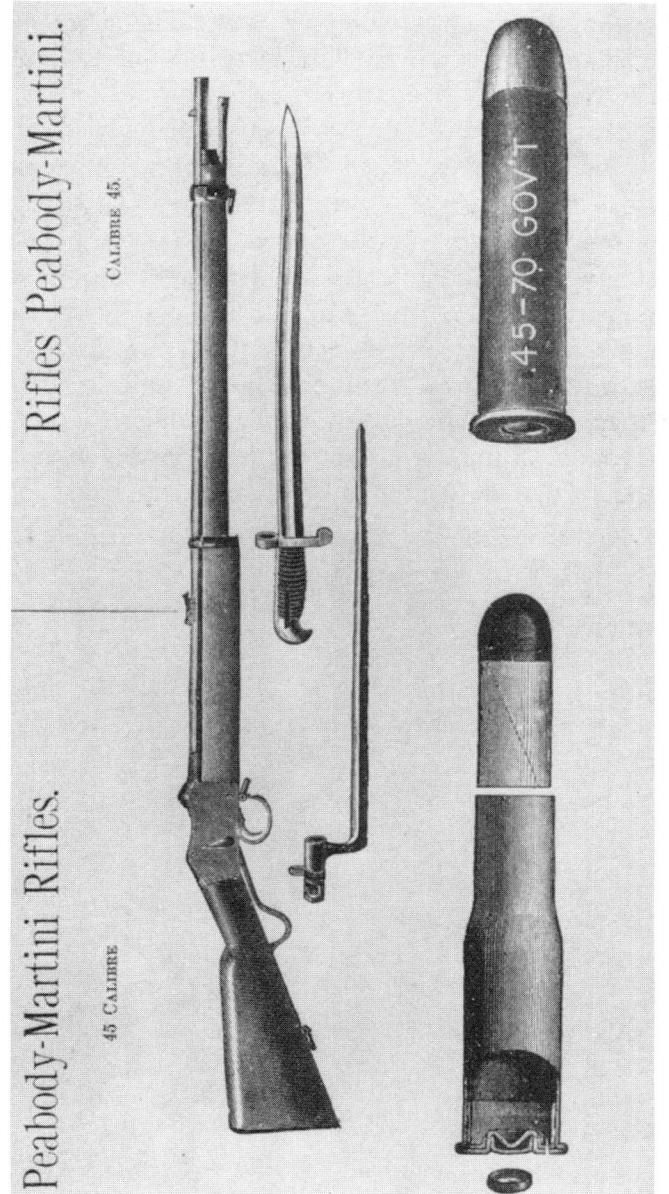

Fig. 79. A Military Peabody Martini rifle.

pears on the stock under the butt plate. The sights are about the mid-range variety. This is truly a fine example of the by-gone days of long range shooting.

It appears that this rifle has been rechambered and possibly rebored by Niedner. Upon examination of the metal forearm tip, it was noted that this tip was shaped to fit the octagon part of the barrel, but as the photograph shows, the octagon part of the barrel is now set back approximately 2 inches behind the end of the tip showing that the barrel has been set back 2 inches.

Most information on Peabody-Martini military rifles show them being made in only foreign calibers, but the author found an illustration in an early Hartley & Graham catalog that shows the military model was available in .45-70 Government, as shown in Fig. 79. As to whether any of these were actually produced is not known.

CHAPTER 9

Maynard

THE FIRST PATENT was issued to Dr. Edward Maynard of Washington, D. C. in May 1851. This was the birth of the famous Maynard rifle, which was to be made by the Massachusetts Arms Co. of Chicopee, Massachusetts. The action of this rifle was operated by an under lever which served as a trigger guard. Downward movement of the lever caused the barrel to tip up and forward exposing the chamber and causing the extractor to pull the cartridge case partly out of the chamber.

As listed in the Maynard Catalog of 1885, the Model 11, the Maynard Improved Hunters' Rifle, the only model chambered for .45-70 caliber was listed as follows:

"THE MAYNARD IMPROVED HUNTERS' RIFLE"

Number Eleven

For large and dangerous games, Model 1873 or Model 1882; .44 caliber, 60, 70 or 100 grains; .45 caliber, 70 grains for U. S. Government Ammunition; .50 caliber, 50, 70 or 100 grains; or .55 caliber, 100 grains; elevat-

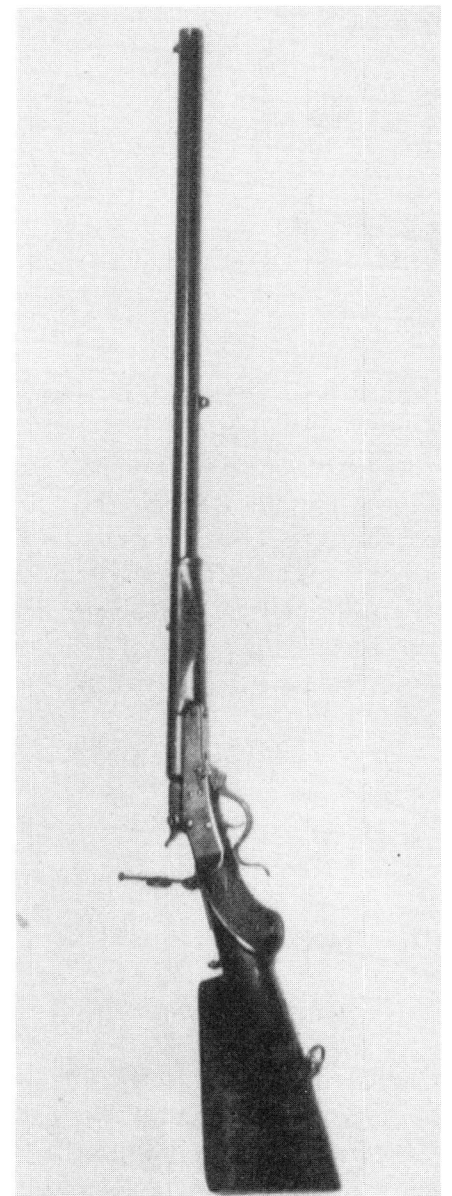

FIG. 80. Number 11 Maynard improved Hunters' rifle.

George Rowbottom Collection

ing graduated peep sight, open hunting sights, plain oil finish stock.

26, 28, 30 or 32 inch barrel	$32.00
Appendages, less shells, bullet mold, loader, loading block, capper, cap picker, rod, brush, rag holder and screw-driver	3.50
Shells for "Model 1873"	$.15 and $.18 cts. each
Shells for "Model 1882"	.08 and .10 cts. each
Mold for express bullet, extra	$3.50

Fig. 80 shows a Number Eleven-Maynard .45-70 caliber rifle in the collection of George Rowbottom.

CHAPTER 10

Whitney

THE WHITNEY Arms Co. was established in Hamden, Connecticut in 1798 by Eli Whitney, Sr., and was operated there until 1888. Whitneys' fame is probably noted mostly for his invention of the cotton gin, but by far his greatest contribution to the world was the manufacture of interchangeable parts. The muskets furnished by Whitney in his first contract, which was completed in 1806, were made by this method, which was unknown in those days. From his genius all our modern manufacturing procedure has been derived.

The Whitney military rifle caliber .45-70 had a rolling block action similar to the Remington previously described. This is described as having a 32½ inch barrel, and the customary full stock. Only a very few were made. A sketch of the Whitney action is shown in Fig. 81. As was common with most manufacturers of that time, a companion carbine was made. This model had a 20½ inch barrel and an overall length of 36 inches, weighing about 7 1/6 pounds.

The more common Whitney is the sporting and target model. This was made in a variety of calibers, among

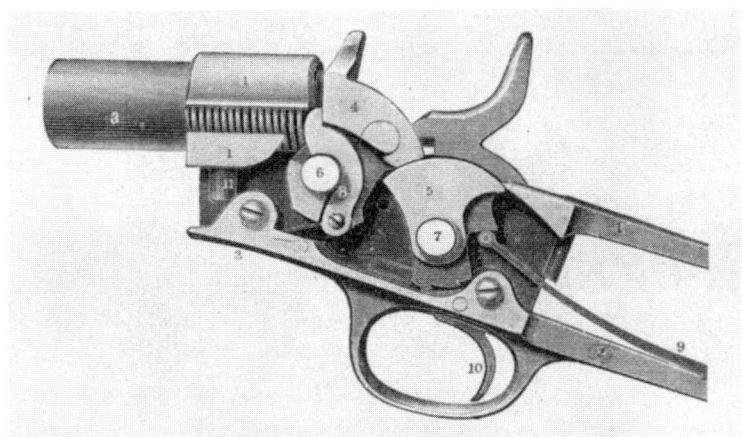

Farrow's Military Encyclopedia
FIG. 81. Cut away view of Whitney rolling block action.

them the .45-70. The action was the same as the military and the weight about 9 to 10 pounds.

Another product of the Whitneyville Armory was the Phoenix rifle, three variations of which are of interest. The military musket is pictured in Fig. 82 and is marked with serial number 3199. The barrel length is 35 inches and weight about 9 pounds.

The corresponding carbine was made with a 20½ inch barrel and weighed 7 pounds. This had the familiar carbine ring on the side of the receiver.

The Phoenix Sporting rifle which was about the same as the military except that it could be furnished with either round or octagon barrels, whereas the military had only round. Barrel lengths varied from 26 to 30 inches.

The model shown in Fig. 83 is serial number 2249, and is in the collection at the Springfield Armory.

The Burgess repeating sporting rifle made by Whitney in .45-70 was very similar in looks to the Winchester lever action. It could be furnished with either round or octagon barrels 28 inches in length. The tubular magazine under the barrel held 9 cartridges. Colt also made Burgess rifles, but these were chambered only for .44-40.

A military rifle was made as above except that the barrel was 33 inches and the magazine held 11 shots. As usual on the military a full stock was applied.

The little brother of the rifle, the military carbine was the same as the rifle except for a 22 inch barrel and a 7 shot magazine.

While on the subject of Whitney, we have shown here in Fig. 84 a very interesting rifle. From all outside appearances it is a Whitney Burgess, but the name Whitney does not appear on it at all. It is marked on the barrel; "G. W. Morse Pat. Oct. 28, 1856," and on the upper tang; "A Burgess Pat. Jan. 7, 1873 and 10/19/75."

At first it was believed this was an experiental model of some sort, except that this rifle bears serial number 1034.

Also, I later ran into another one in the 500 numbers and there is also one on display in the Winchester museum.

Although, this volume is not meant to cover experimental arms, another unusual piece in the author's collection should be mentioned here as it has all the earmarks of Burgess.

The double shown in Fig. 85, page 103, is a combination 16 gauge shotgun and .45-70 rifle.

This combination gun bears no name on it at all. The only markings are a letter "B" and a "2" on each hammer. It appears to have never been fully completed and never blued. Besides being a combination gun, it is

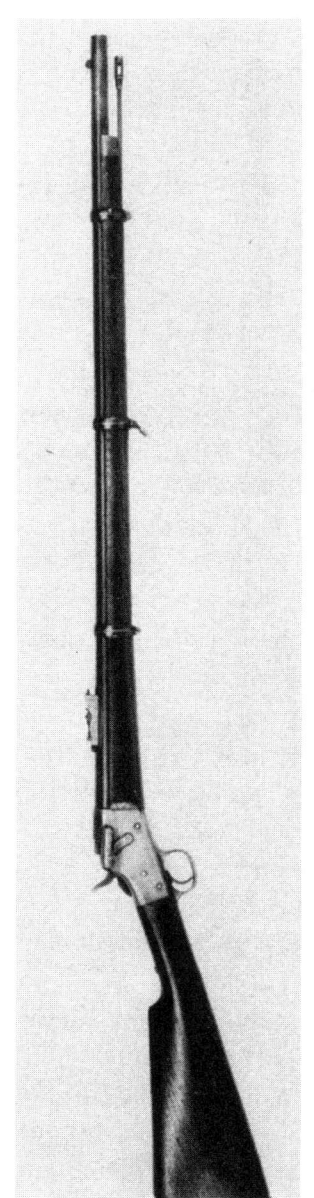

Courtesy of Winchester-Western Division Olin Mathieson Chemical Corporation

FIG. 82. Phoenix Military single shot musket.

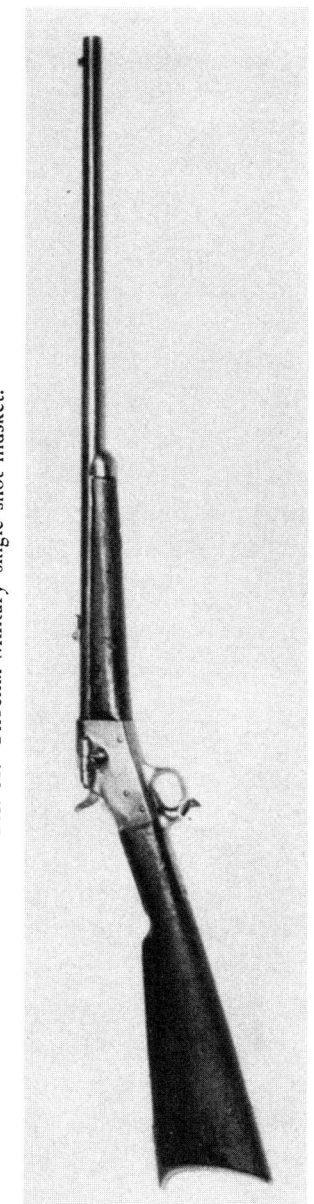

Springfield Armory

FIG. 83. Phoenix single shot Sporting rifle. Serial number 2249.

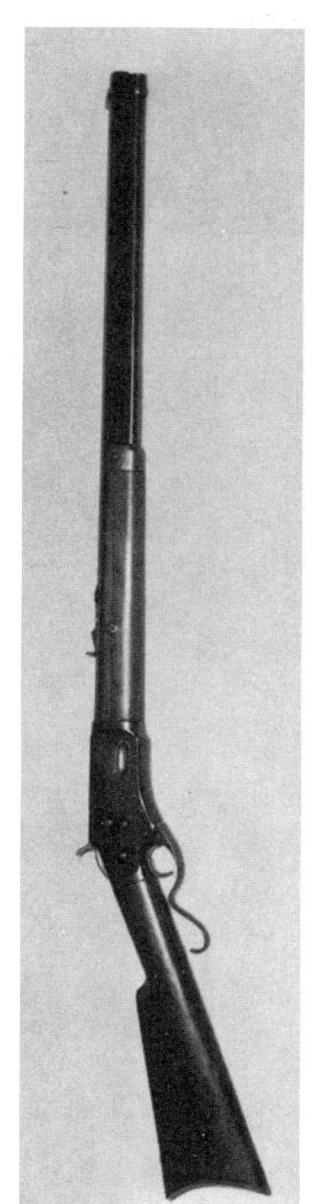

Fig. 84. Whitney Burgess repeating rifle.

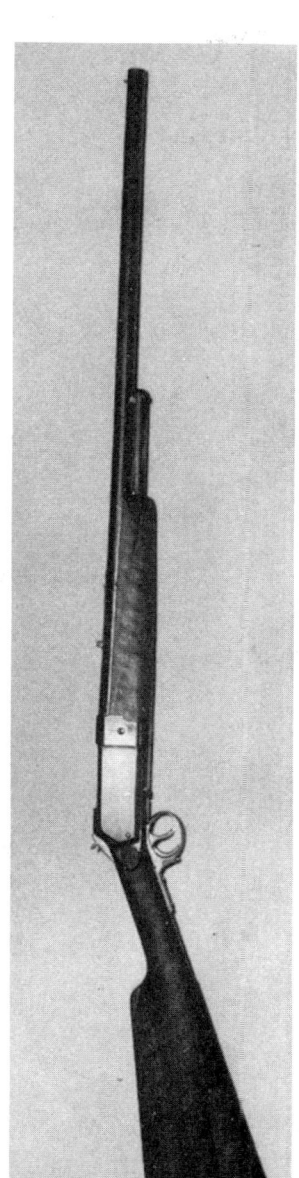

Fig. 85. A Burgess experimental combination 16 gauge shotgun and .45-70 rifle.

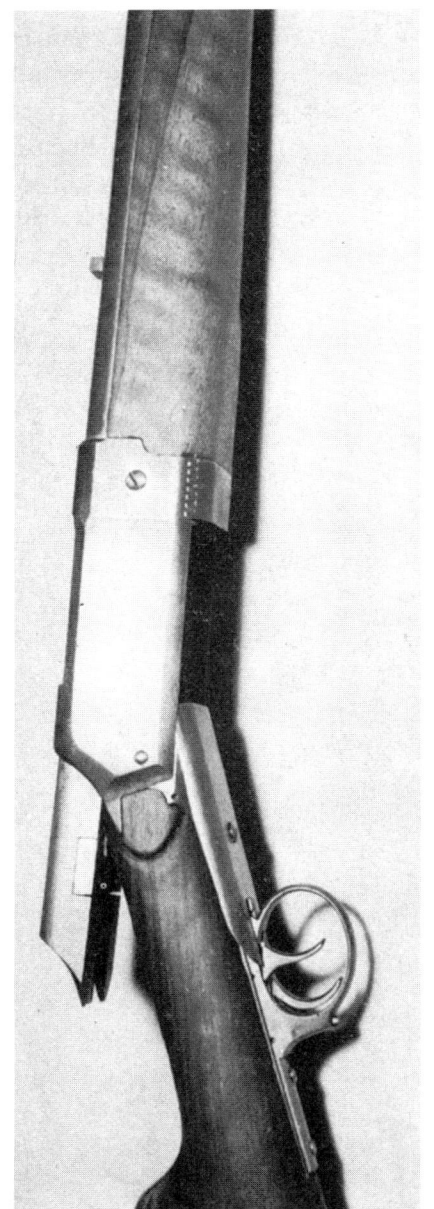

FIG. 86. The open action of the experimental Burgess.

a magazine gun, as there are two separate tubular magazines in the fore-arm. The one for the shotshell holds one cartridge, and the one for the .45-70 four cartridges. The action is operated by pressing a button on the trigger guard and pulling to the rear; this causes the trigger guard to slide backward, and unlocks the breech which also slides rearward, cocking the hammers as it does so (Fig. 86).

Upon examination of this unusual mechanism, it seems to have no provision to hold the unfired cartridges of either barrel in place, if only one is fired and the receiver opened. If anyone can bring more light on this rifle. I would be more than grateful.

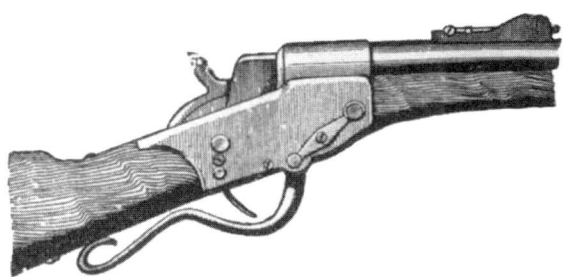

Francis Bannerman's Catalog

FIG. 87. The Buck single shot rifle.

CHAPTER 11

Miscellaneous Makers

IT IS BELIEVED we have now covered all arms made by the larger manufacturers in the latter part of the nineteenth century. In this the final chapter on rifles will be explained as well as possible the lesser known arms of the .45-70 caliber.

The H. A. Buck & Co. of West Stafford, Connecticut, made a single shot rifle about 1880. A Buck rifle is shown in Fig. 87. This rifle was a lever action of the falling block type; the lever used to operate the action served as the trigger guard similar to the Winchester single shot. The Buck was submitted to the Springfield armory board, but did not meet with approval, and the company soon went out of business.

The Overbaugh target rifle was made in about 1887 and is believed to have been a rolling block type of action. Barrel lengths were 28 to 30 inches and weights were from 8½ to 10 pounds.

Another arm of vague description is the Hotchkiss Model 1875 single shot military rifle. Evidently this piece was not made by Winchester. No details are available.

The Russell Magazine Gun was invented by Lieut. A. H. Russell, Ordnance Corps., U.S.A. A picture of

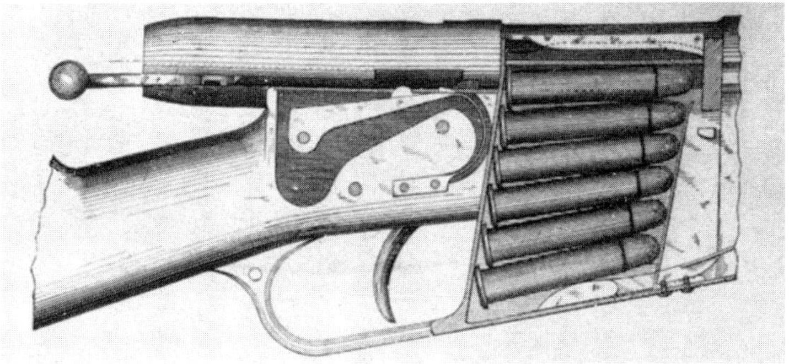

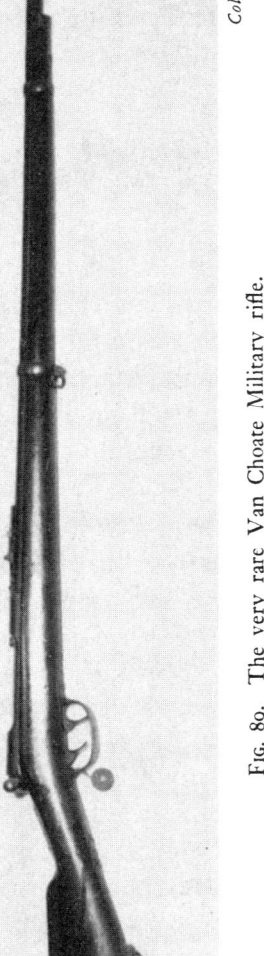

Farrow's Military Encyclopedia

FIG. 88. The action of the Russell rifle partly cut away.

Colt Museum

FIG. 89. The very rare Van Choate Military rifle.

108

this arm is shown in Fig. 88. The Russell is of the bolt action variety with a box magazine in front of the trigger guard, (Fig. 88). The movement of the bolt is not a rotating motion, but a straight pull to the rear. Upon closing the bolt a cross-shaft in the bolt with cam shaped ends seats into recesses in either side of the receiver. No description as to lengths and weights of the Russell have been found by the author.

To say the Van Choate rifle is rare, is a gross understatement. Although Satterlee lists the Van Choate, the only specimen the writer has ever seen is on display at the Colt Museum and is pictured in Fig. 89. The rifle is a single shot bolt action type with set triggers. Barrel length is 32 inches. It is marked; Van-Choate Pat. Brown Mfg. Co., Newburyport, Mass. Another name for the Van-Choate was the "Brown Bolt" gun.

A sporting version of the Ward Burton in caliber .45-70 was made with magazines to hold 3 to 8 cartridges. This was the same bolt action as the military rifles and carbines made at the Springfield Armory in 1871. Details on the commercial model are lacking.

Martin Rywell lists in his book "American Antique Rifles and Their Current Prices" two arms in .45-70 upon which the writer can find no other information to confirm or deny their existence. The first of these is the Charles Foehl hammerless target rifle made by the Deringer Rifle and Pistol Works, Philadelphia, Pennsylvania. This had a 28 inch part round and part octagon barrel and double set triggers. Patent dates were June 25, 1876, and May 14, 1879. Secondly was the Jacobs .45-70 double rifle made also in Philadelphia, Pa., no further description is available.

While on the subject of double rifles, Fig. 90 illus-

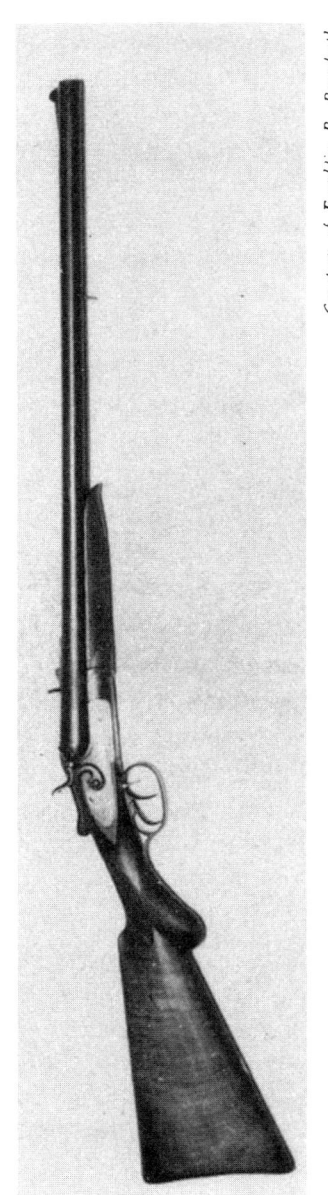

Fig. 90. Greener Double rifle.

Courtesy of Franklin B. Brandreth

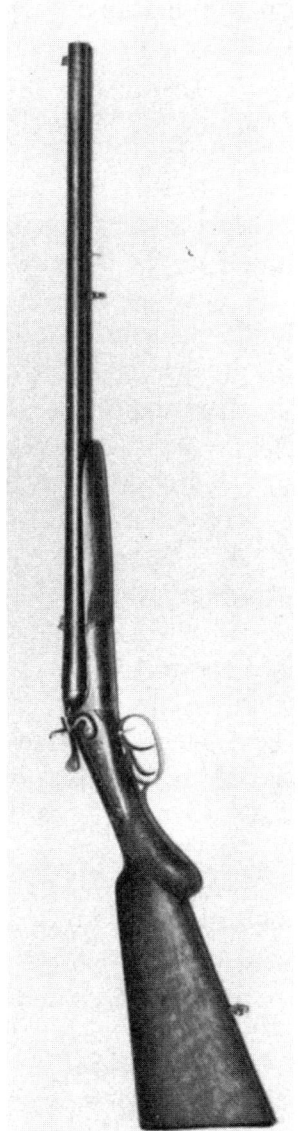

Fig. 91a. A 12 gauge double shotgun relined with .45-70 rifle barrels.

Author's Collection

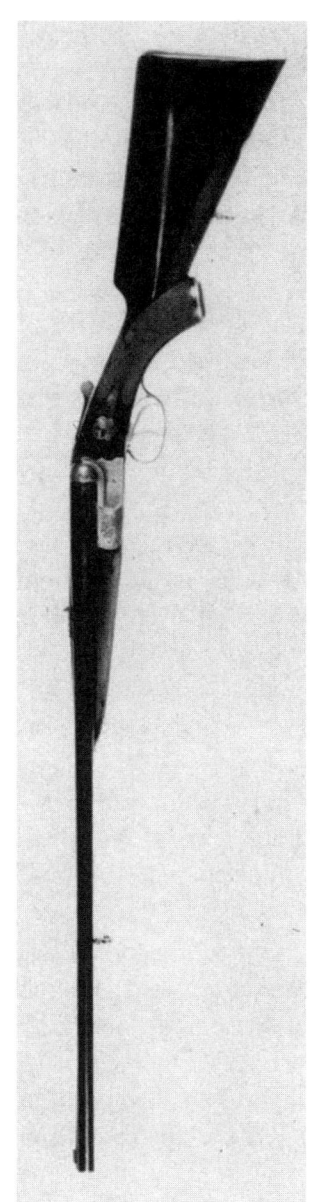

FIG. 91b. A 16 gauge double shotgun relined to .45-70 by the author.

Author's Collection

trates one of the finest I have seen. It is an FH.60 grade W. W. Greener with Whitworth steel barrels in (naturally) .45-70 caliber. According to Greener this arm was built in 1903 and is described as having "a flat engine turned rib, full pistol grip hand stock, sling eyes and has one stand and two leaf back sights, platina tipped bead foresight and when sold was complete in a leather box case."

The double rifle in this caliber is one of our rarest guns and always will demand top prices. In view of this, I have never been able to obtain one for my personal collection, but pictured here in Figs. 91a and 91b is a pair of .45-70 doubles made from 12 and 16 gauge shotguns.

These were made by the writer in his own shop. The job was accomplished by turning new 1884 Springfield barrels and lining the shotgun barrels with them. The liners are a drive fit to the entire length of the barrels and are also held by set screws under the barrels just forward of the chambers. Naturally a new extractor had to be made.

Actually the two double rifles have no direct bearing on this story and are only shown as a curiosity. Both have been fired by the author, but accuracy is nothing to brag about.

The sole surviving .45-70 still in production is the Harrington & Richardson line throwing gun. This is not a rifle, as it is smoothbore and fires a .45-70 blank cartridge. From all outward appearances Harrington & Richardson have used their single barrel tip-up hammer shot gun action and fitted to it a 14¼ inch .45 caliber smooth bore barrel.

According to information received from Harrington

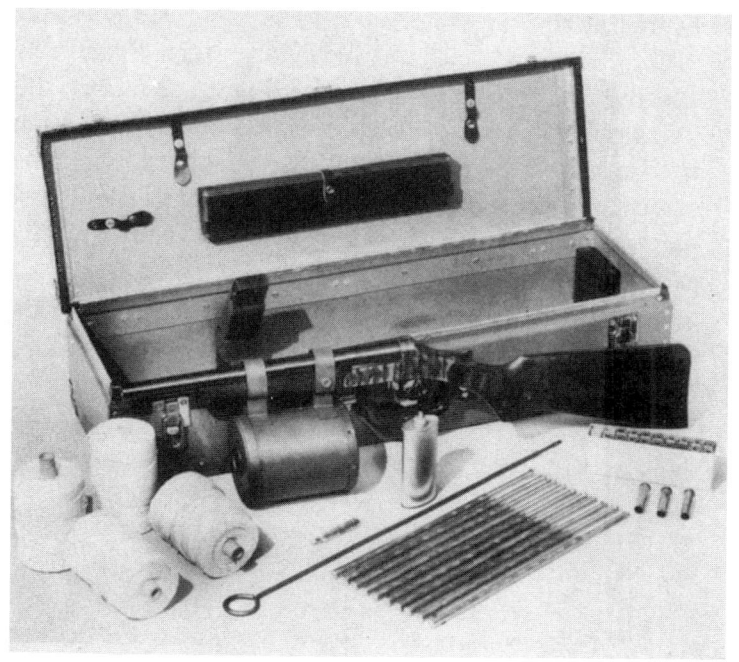

Courtesy of Harrington & Richardson
Fig. 92. A Harrington & Richardson line throwing gun with complete accessories.

& Richardson this gun was first made in 1940 for the U. S. Government, although now Harrington & Richardson have a nice business making them for fire departments, steamship lines, logging companies, etc. Fig. 92 is a photo of the complete line-throwing Gun Kit, supplied through the courtesy of Harrington & Richardson.

Harrington & Richardson also manufactured at the turn of the century a .45-70 shotgun. This was built on their regular tip-up shot gun action. The barrel length was 26 inches. The one shown in Fig. 94 is owned by George Rowbottom of Hamden, Connecticut and is serial number 1930.

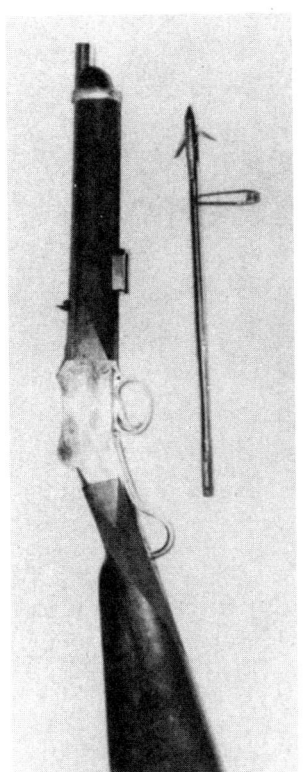
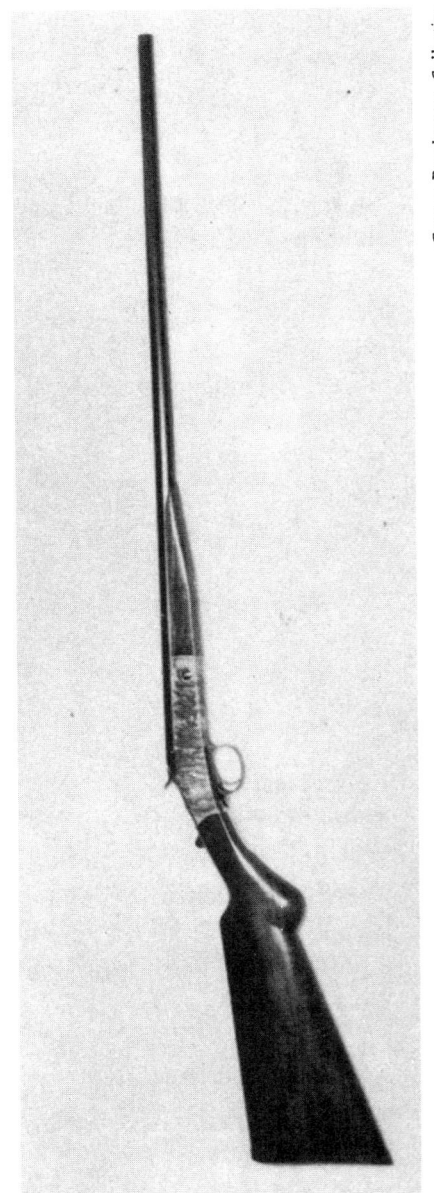

Fig. 93. Gastinne-Rennette .45-70 harpoon gun.

An unusual gun is Fig. 93. This is not a rifle, but a smooth-bore harpoon gun. It is marked 'Fini Par Gastinne-Rennette." and stamped .45-70 on the barrel. The barrel is 13 1/8 inches long and the accompanying harpoon is 15 ¾ inches long. This arm as shown here seems to be completely original in every respect from the British martini-action to the short forearm and short barrel. You will note on the underside of the forearm is an adapter that most likely filled into a deck-mount of some kind. Any further information on this gun would be appreciated.

In the Springfield Armory Museum are a pair of pistols made from 1868 trap-door muskets chambered for the .50-70 cartridge. Made up strictly on an experimental basis, and only two were made, so never buy one.

When the writer heard of these pistols, he figured why not .45-70? So on a cold rainy Sunday afternoon he retired to his shop in the cellar. The result is shown in Fig. 95. It was made from an 1884 Springfield rifle with the barrel and stock cut off and the pistol grip added to the stock. The gun has been fired with special reduced loads and accuracy at 25 yards was not too bad.

All of this proves nothing and has only been included to more or less round out the story.

CHAPTER 12

Automatic Field Pieces

ALTHOUGH THIS narrative, by nature of its title deals with rifles, in this the final chapter on arms we will leave the rifle and discuss the early machine gun. Actually the three weapons to be explained here are not true machine guns as they are all manually operated and probably would be properly called "Battery" guns.

It was just as important in the time when the .45-70 was our service cartridge, to have interchangeable ammunition as it is today. Therefore, with the invention of the automatic field piece, it was chambered for the then standard .45-70 rifle shell.

The most widely used machine gun of the time was the Gatling. Although the variations of this arm were many, there were actually two basic models, one with 5 barrels and one with 10. Each barrel had its own lock.

The operation of this piece was accomplished by the gunner turning a crank. The turning of the crank caused the barrels to revolve around a central axis. The cartridges were fed from a magazine located over the rear of the barrels. As the crank was turned and the barrels revolved each breech passing under the magazine allowed the cartridge to drop into it.

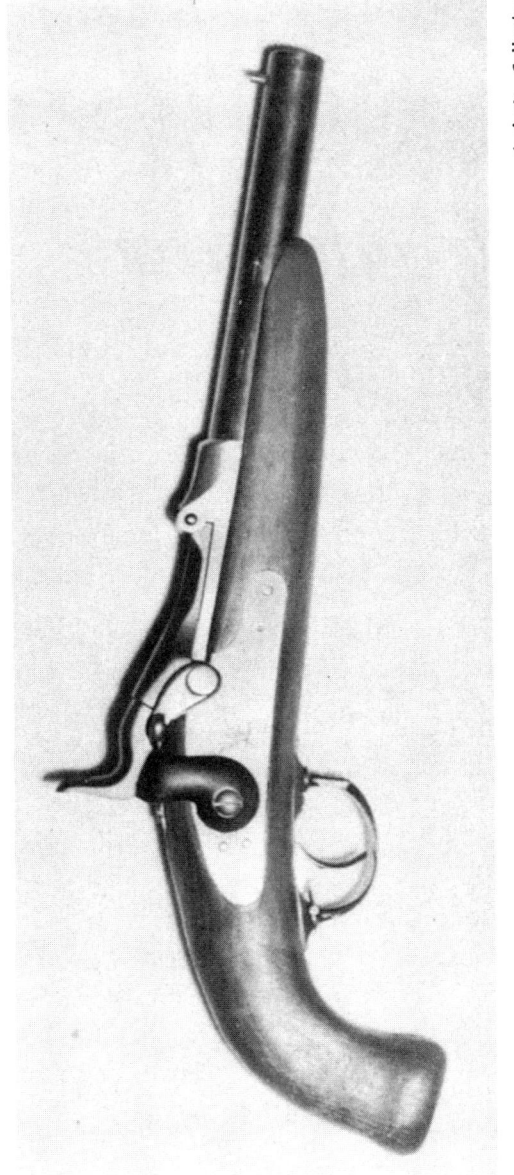

Fig. 95. A .45-70 trap door pistol made from an 1884 Springfield rifle.

Author's Collection

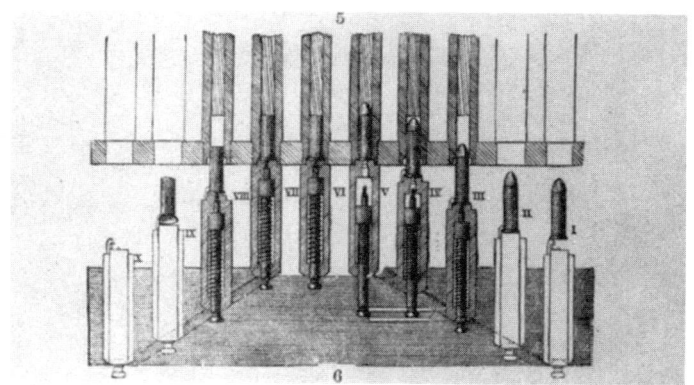

Farrow's Military Encyclopedia
FIG. 96. The cam ring of a Gatling Gun.

The cartridge was then carried in the breech and through a cam action was forced into the chamber automatically fired, and it was ready to receive a new shell.

A picture of the cam ring is shown in Fig. 96. The magazine for the Gatling consisted of a vertical tube in which the cartridges were stacked and fed by gravity into the feed mechanism. A later and improved type called the "Accles positive drum-type magazine" was said to have been able to fire up to 1200 shots per minute.

The three basic models shown here are as follows: Fig. 97, an 1875 ten barreled type on tripod, marked serial number 110 New Jersey. This one is in the Winchester collection.

Fig. 98 illustrates the Model 1883, five barrel type. This one is the light weight version adapted for being carried by mules or camels.

The final Gatling shown in Fig. 99 mounted on a carriage is the 10 barrel, Model 1883 with the Accles feed.

The following information on the Gardner machine

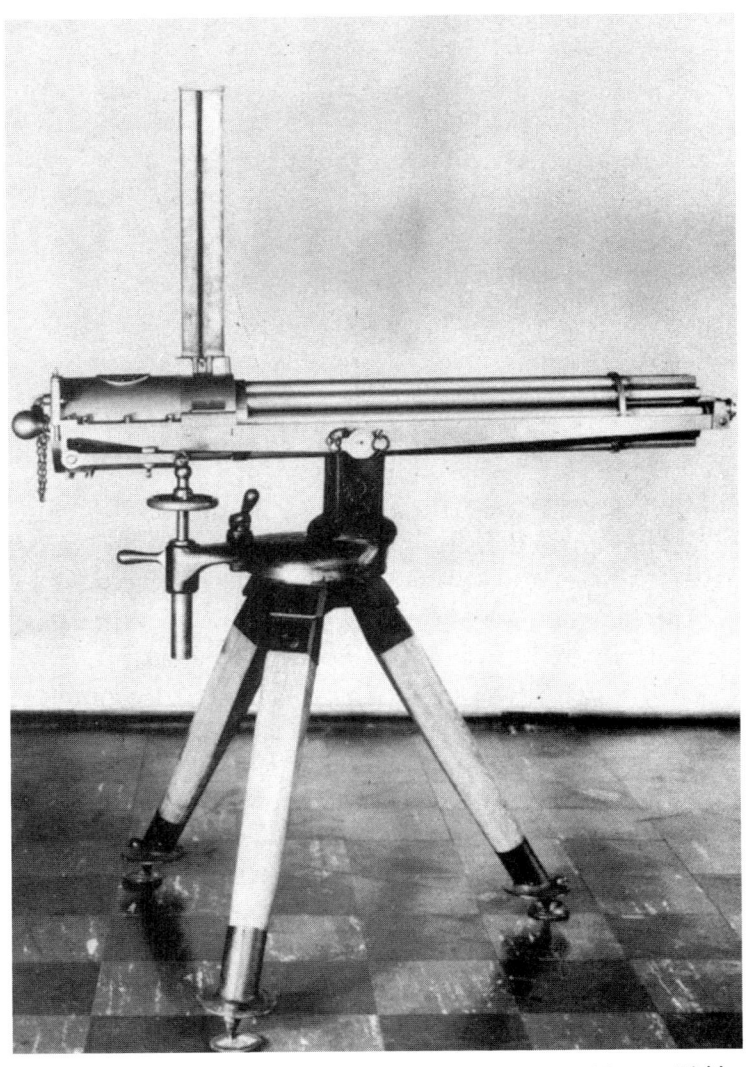

*Courtesy of Winchester-Western Division
Olin Mathieson Chemical Corporation*

FIG. 97. The 1875 10 barrel Gatling gun. Serial number 110.

Farrow's Military Encyclopedia

FIG. 98. An 1883 5 barrel Gatling on tripod.

gun has been compiled from two reliable sources namely: *Farrows Military Encyclopedia* and *The Machine Gun* Volume 1 by Chinn. These references are necessary as the writer has never had the opportunity to examine a Gardner.

Two barrels firing alternately by rotating a crank cover is the basic operation of this arm. The internal works of the Gardner consisted of a crankshaft with two crankpins; to each was connected the bolt for each barrel. As the crankpins were 180° apart one revolution

Farrow's Military Encyclopedia
FIG. 99. An 1883 10 barrel Gatling on carriage.

Farrow's Military Encyclopedia
FIG. 100a. A 2 barrel Gardner mounted on field carriage.

of the shaft would load and fire each barrel. To feed two barrels, a vertical feed tube with two "T" slots was used. To ease loading, the cartridges were first loaded into special wooden blocks with the rim end protruding. This enabled the loader to slide the cartridges in the feed tube "T" slots and remove the block.

William Gardner, the inventor, not being able to finance production of his gun, sold the American Patent rights to Pratt & Whitney of Hartford, Connecticut.

After several tests it was recommended that the War Department purchase a limited number to be put into field use, but nothing ever actually developed.

The British purchased the manufacturing rights from Pratt & Whitney and built a factory for its manufacture on the basis that Gardner would go to England to supervise its construction. The inventor agreed and remained in that country until his death. Shown on a field carriage in Fig. 100a is Gardner machine gun.

The final type of machine gun we will discuss is the Lowell Battery Gun, invented by DeWitt Clinton Farrington in 1875. According to Col. Chinn, the Lowell was manufactured by the Lowell Mfg. Company, Lowell, Mass. The only two specimens the author has seen were marked "Ames Mfg. Co., Chicopee, Mass." These two, one of which is in the author's collection, and the other belongs to William Ruger, are serial numbers 160 and 163.

The Lowell is unusual, in that it has 4 barrels mounted in a circle around a common axis, and fires only one of the 4 barrels, the other 3 being held in reserve. When the barrel in use becomes heated, a lever at the rear of the barrel is moved and the overheated barrel is rotated to one side and a cool one takes its place.

Courtesy *West Point Museum*

Fig. 100b. Gardner Machine Gun as made by Pratt & Whitney, Hartford, Conn., Model 1879.

A "T" slot-type vertical magazine is used in the Lowell also. The cartridges are gravity fed from the magazine into a feed roll. The feed roll has slots milled into it to receive the ammunition and it is rotated as the crank is turned. The crank being located directly at the rear of the gun. As the crank is rotated, the feed roll indexes and alignes the cartridge with the open end of the barrel.

Upon further movement of the crank the bolt moves forward pushing the shell into the barrel. The motion of the bolt is accomplished by a large rotary drum which has two grooves cut in it. One groove is cut so as to engage a lug on the rear of the bolt, move it forward, hold it in place while firing and withdraw it, extracting the spent case. A second lug on the bottom of the bolt

FIG. 101. A view of a Lowell battery gun with the cover open to expose the mechanism. *Author's Collection*

Farrow's Military Encyclopedia
FIG. 102. A Lowell battery gun on field carriage.

FIG. 103. The author firing his Lowell battery gun.

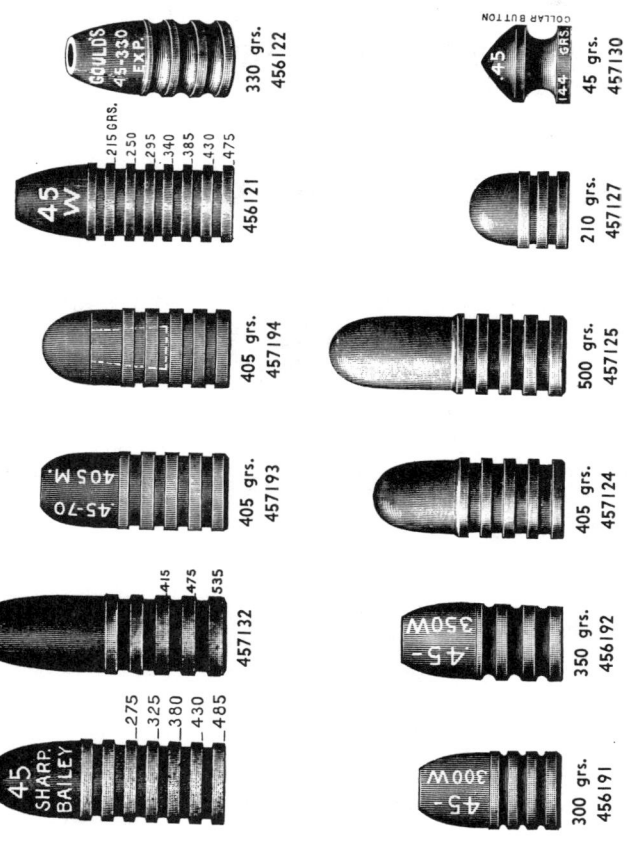

Fig. 104. Lymann Ideal bullets.

Courtesy of Lymann Gunsight Company

engaged in the second groove, compresses and releases the firing pin spring. A steel lock on the drum comes into position just before the firing pin is released. The bolt then remains locked from approximately 30° of rotation to lessen danger from hang-fires.

For cleaning and inspection, the entire top cover is hinged and upon opening, all major parts are exposed. Also the barrels, being mounted on a trunion at the front may be tipped up for examination. Fig. 101 shows a Lowell in this condition.

The next two pictures illustrate the Lowell mounted on a carriage (Fig. 102) and on a tripod (Fig. 103).

In actual trials the Lowell showed up very favorably, but the Gatling was too well established, the country was at peace, and there was no foreseeable trouble in the near future. A few were purchased by the navy, three by California for prison use, and one by the City of Cincinnati. A final illustration for the story of the .45-70 is a picture of the author test firing his Lowell battery gun.

CHAPTER 13

Handloading the .45-70

SHOWN HERE is probably the most complete listing of hand loads of .45-70 ever assembled. None of these loads are the author's. The information has come from the following three sources: *Complete Guide to Hand Loading*, by Phil Sharpe, *Ideal Handbook No. 39* and *American Rifleman*, November, 1950.

Inasmuch as hand loading is always a delicate subject, caution cannot be overemphasized. It must be remembered the .45-70 was a black powder cartridge and practically all rifles chambered for it are in the low pressure category.

The first and foremost of these is the trapdoor Springfield for which pressures must *definitely be kept under 25,000 lbs.* In no case should pressures exceed this amount and it is particularly important to play safe and keep them below this maximum. It is also well to consider all other rifles in this same class with the exception of the 1886 Winchester, the single shot high-wall Winchester, and the Sharps Bouchardt. Even on these three, unless they have a nickel steel barrel, black powder is preferable. Though the action will stand the pressure of smokeless powder, the high temperatures developed will erode soft steel barrels just forward of the chamber. Jacketed bullets should be used only in nickel barrels as they too, are destructive to the bore of soft steel. Please remember the loads shown here are reprinted and are definitely not recommendations of the author who would assume no responsibility as to the performance or safety of any of them.

As for the brass, Elmer Keith, who is also a .45-70 fan and has helped the writer tremendously in preparing this work, has advised that the best brass to use when available are the old tin plated Frankford Arsenal cases. With this point, I fully agree as the Frankford cases are much thicker just forward of the rim and do not have the recess under the rim as do modern cases. That there is more metal in these cases is easily noticeable if you should ever try to full length resize one.

The bullets available for loading are numerous ranging from 215 grain "collar button" through 500 grain arsenal bullet. For long range target shooting, the 500 grain is more stable and wind has very little effect on it.

For general purpose all-round use, either the 300 or 405 grain is usually preferred—the 300 grain particularly as it has a much lighter recoil and does not empty your lead pot as fast when casting them. In most cases the lead bullets sized to .457 are satisfactory, but if you want real accuracy, the bore of your pet gun should be slugged and measured and the bullets sized accordingly. As for primers, either the Remington 9½ or Winchester 120 have been found completely satisfactory.

In closing, I leave here enough hand loads to keep the gun crank busy loading for a long time and with the final remark, *be careful.*

Loading Data from *Complete Guide to Handloading*, by Sharpe

Since this was at one time a government rifle cartridge, a great deal of handloading data has been prepared with it. Most guns will not stand over 25,000 pounds pressure safely, since the cartridge was essentially of the black powder era. The army used it only in single shot rifles of various makes and styles and with various charges of powders and weights of bullets. The heaviest load for it was the .45-70-500, in which 70 grains of black powder were used to drive a 500 grain pure lead bullet. Later the bullet weight was cut to 405 grains, and the smokeless jacketed bullet loading in the high velocity type uses the 300 grain bullet. Various other weights have been tried with reasonable success. The cartridge can be handloaded to excellent accuracy with both jacketed and cast bullet. When loading for the old-timers, however, one must bear in mind that smokeless powders with jacketed bullets are extremely dangerous and destructive to the barrel.

.45-70

Bullet			Powder		Ballistics		
Weight in grains	Type style make	Seating depth	Kind	Weight charge grains	MV in 26 inch barrel	Breech pressure	Recommended by
240	Lead	.272	Unique	15.0	1648	12,300	Her.
240	Lead	.272	Unique	20.8	1972	24,000	Her.
240	Lead	.250	SR 80	19.0	1115	.....	Du P
240	Lead	.250	SR 80	29.0	1630	.....	Du P
300	SP	.430	2400	24.0	1560	13,500	Her.
300	SP	.430	2400	30.6	1905	24,000	Her.
300	SP	.430	Unique	13.0	1330	12,000	Her.
300	SP	.430	Unique	18.7	1685	24,000	Her.
300	SP	.430	Sharpshooter	20.0	1420	.....	Her.
300	SP	.430	Sharpshooter	30.0	1960	22,800	Her.
300	SP	.430	Sharpshooter	34.0	2125	30,000	Her.
300	SP	.430	Lightning	25.0	1320	.....	....

.45—70

Bullet			Powder		Ballistics		Recommended by
Weight in grains	Type style make	Seating depth	Kind	Weight charge grains	MV in 26 inch barrel	Breech pressure	
300	SP	.430	Lightning	35.0	1760	17,400	Her.
300	SP	.430	Lightning	44.0	2125	30,000	Her.
300	SP	.430	Hi Vel 2	48.0	1921[1]	26,000	Her.
300	SP	.430	Her.300	54.0	1875[1]	27,000	Her.
300	SP	.430	Her.300	60.0	2050[1]	32,000	Her.
300	SP	.450	3031	48.0	1675	.....	Du P
300	SP	.450	3031	58.0	2015	.....	Du P
300	SP	.400	17½	51.0	1700	.....	Du P
300	SP	.400	17½	55.7	1875	.....	Du P
300	SP	.400	17½	59.0	2015	.....	Du P
300	SP	.400	SR 80	25.0	1565	.....	Du P
300	SP	.400	SR 80	35.0	1800[1]	.....	Du P
300	SP	.400	18	50.0	1800[1]	.....	Du P
300	SP	.400	18	54.0	1925[1]	.....	Du P
300	SP	.400	16	48.0	1780	.....	Du P
300	SP	.400	16	50.7	1890	23,000	Du P
300	SP	.400	16	56.0	2140	32,000	Du P
344	Lead	.417	Unique	14.0	1335	11,700	Her.
344	Lead	.417	Unique	19.2	1598	24,000	Her.
379	Lead	.450	SR 80	21.0	1115	.....	Du P
379	Lead	.450	SR 80	29.0	1450	.....	Du P
405	SP	.572	2400	22.0	1290	14,000	Her.
405	SP	.572	2400	27.4	1560	24,000	Her.
405	SP	.572	Sharpshooter	18.0	1165	.....	Her.
405	SP	.572	Sharpshooter	24.0	1460	18,500	Her.
405	SP	.572	Sharpshooter	30.2	1730	30,000	Her.
405	SP	.572	Lightning	25.0	1200	.....	Her.
405	SP	.572	Lightning	31.0	1440	18,400	Her.
405	SP	.572	Lightning	39.0	1760	30,000	Her.
405	SP	.572	Pyro	44.0	1500[1]	23,000	....
405	SP	.572	Pyro	49.0	1700[1]	32,000	....
405	Lead	.535	Unique	11.0	1133	12,300	Her.
405	Lead	.535	Unique	17.3	1472	24,000	Her.
405	Lead	.535	Sharpshooter	20.0	1280[2]	.....	Her.
405	Lead	.625	1204	28.5	1375	.....	Du P
405	Lead	.625	1204	35.0	1550	.....	Du P
405	Lead	.625	DI rifle	32.0	....	.....	Du P
405	Lead	.625	SR 80	17.0	1050	.....	Du P
500	Lead	.564	Unique	11.0	1020	11,600	Her.
500	Lead	.564	Unique	17.2	1330	24,000	Her.
500	Lead	.564	Sharpshooter	23.2	1330	18,000	Her.
500	Lead	.564	Fg. black	70.0	1320	25,000	Her.

[1] Velocity with corrosive primer.
[2] Estimated velocity.

CHART FROM *IDEAL HANDBOOK NO. 38*

Bullet	Grain weight	Powder	Charge grain weight	Muzzle velocity F.S.	Remarks
		Loads for cast bullets			
		(Safe for Springfield and other weaker .45-70 rifles)			
457129	146	#6 pistol	5.0	950E	Rd. Ball
457130	144	Unique	5.0	900E	Collar button bullet
457127	210	Bulk shotgun	6.5	1000E	Very mild
457127	210	Unique	7.0	....	
456191	300	#2400	20.0	1325	Good
456191	300	#4759	26.0	1375	Good
456121	340	#2400	20.0	1300	Accurate
457124	405	#4759	20.0	867	Very mild
457124	405	{ FFg[a] { #6 pistol	62.0 } 8.0 }	1400E	Put black powder in last. Enough so that bullet compresses powder charge. Burns clean.
		Loads for jacketed bullets			
Jacketed	300	#4759	25.0	1565	
Jacketed	300	#3031	48.0	1675	
Jacketed	300	#2400	30.6	1905	
Jacketed	300	Unique	18.7	1685	
Jacketed	405	#4198	36.0	1417	Remington S.P. bullet

[a] 62 Grains FFg may be varied to obtain correct bulk in case.

TABLE FROM *AMERICAN RIFLEMAN*, NOVEMBER, 1950

TABLE 1

Pressure and velocity for .45-70 in older rifles

Load	Weight grains	Bullet type	Bullet dia. (inch)	Seating depth (inch)	Powder charge grains	Powder type	Lot no. of primer	Case make	Vel.	Pressure
1	210	Ideal 457127	.457	.26	30.0	Fg black	WRA120	Western	1032	.....[4]
2	500	Ideal 457125	.457	.63	70.0	Fg black	WRA120	Western	1112	15,900[5]
3	300	Ideal 456191	.457	.40	35.0	Lightning	West 8½	Western	1627	17,075[6]
4	300	Ideal 456191	.457	.40	26.0	4759	Rem. 9½	Remington	1375	.....[7]
5	405	Ideal 457124	.457	.55	20.0	4759	Rem. 9½	Remington	867	.....[7]
6	405	Rem. S.P.	.458	.55	36.0	4198	Rem. 8½	Remington	1417	.....[7]
7	405	Ideal 457124	.457	.55	50.0	Fg black	West 8½	Western	968	.....[7]

TABLE 2

Pressure and velocity for .45-70 in modern rifles

Load	Weight grains	Bullet type	Bullet dia. (inch)	Seating depth (inch)	Powder charge grains	Powder type	Lot no. of primer	Case make	Vel.	Pressure
1	405	Rem. S.P.	.458	.55	17.5	Unique	—WRA120	Western	1286	25,240[8]
2	405	Rem. S.P.	.458	.55	30.0	Lightning	—West 8½	Western	1257	17,220[8]
3	405	Rem. S.P.	.458	.55	27.4	#2400	—West 8½	Western	1827	21,460[8]
4	405	Rem. S.P.	.458	.55	53.0	3031	—	Remington	1827	28,933[8]
5	405	Ideal 457124	.457	.55	53.0	3031	97 WRA120	Western	1871	29,220[8]
6	405	Commercial load	...	.	...	...	....	....	1364	20,200[8]

[4] Light load.
[5] O.K.
[6] Maximum.
[7] Mild load.
[8] For 1886 Winchester.

Appendix

Cartridge Interchangeability

It has been suggested by my friend, Bill Ruger, that the readers might be interested in a brief note on the interchangeability of the .45-70 cartridge.

Although today it is manufactured in one load only, in the past, the shooter had many variations from which to choose. These range from the ".45-5-140 Government Armory Practice" through the .45-85-290 Bullard, all of which were loaded in the same case, the case being 2-1/10 inches long. Although the cartridge boxes were marked to show the load contained in them, the cartridges were all headstamped .45-70 with the exception of the .45-85 Marlin, the .45-85 Colt, and the .45-85 Bullard, which were so marked.

Below, I have tried to list as many as possible of these different cartridges that have the 2-1/10 inch case length and may be fired in any rifle marked ".45-70" or ".45 Government" or the three ".45-85's" listed. (This does not include the ".45-85" Winchester which is a 2-4/10 inch case length.)

2 1/10 Inch Case Length

.45-5 -140	Government Armory Practice
.45-15-230	Government Armory Practice
.45-25-300	Government Carbine Practice
.45-20-230	Government Armory Practice
.45-35-365	Government Armory Practice
.45-55-405	Government Carbine Practice

.45-70-405	Government
.45-70-500	Government (New Model)
.45-70-420	Sharps Straight
.45-70-357	Sharps Express Straight
.45-70-405	Marlin Magazine
.45-70-330	Gould (hollow Point)
.45-85-285	Marlin Magazine
.45-85-290	Colt
.45-85-290	Bullard Rifle

After listing the above, it also seems necessary to give the reader a list of rifles that are marked other than ".45-70" or ".45 Government" in which the .45-70 cartridge may be successfully fired. By successfully, it is meant that the chamber would be the same with the exception that it would be of longer length. Virtually, the same relation as between a .22 short and .22 long. This will enable the reader to fire the relatively plentiful and inexpensive .45-70 cartridge in rifles that otherwise require the consumption of some of these extremely rare old cartridges, some of which incidentally would be made for the use of Berden Primers. If this information would enable at least one shooter to dust off a fine old Sharps Rifle and spend an afternoon of pleasant, although not extremely accurate shooting, it will be more than worthwhile.

Bullet	Make	Model	Case Length
.45-82 -405	Winchester		2 4/10 inches
.45-85 -350	Winchester		2 4/10 inches
.45-85 -300	Winchester	& Express	2 4/10 inches
.45-90 -300	Winchester	& Marlin Model	2 4/10 inches
.45-90 -500	Sharps	Straight	2 6/10 inches
.45-105-550	Sharps	Straight	2 7/8 inches
.45-120-550	Sharps	Straight	3 1/4 inches
.45-125-500	Sharps	Straight	3 1/4 inches

Most of the above cartridge specifications have been obtained from the Union Metallic Cartridge Company listing in the M. Hartley Company Catalog of 1903.

Bibliography

The Beechloader in the Service, Fuller.
The Rifle in America, Sharpe.
Farrow's Military Encyclopedia, Farrow.
Francis P. Bannerman's Catalog—1936.
U. S. Muskets, Rifles & Carbines, Gluckman.
Fourteen Old Gun Catalogs, Satterlee.
Hartley & Graham Catalog—1888.
M. Hartley Catalog—1903.
Schoverling, Daly & Gales Catalog—1904.
Single Shot Rifles, Jame J. Grant.
American Antique Rifles & Their Current Prices.
    Martin Rywell.
Firearms in the Custer Battle, Parsons & duMont.
Colts Double Rifles, Fred Mills.
Rules & Management, Springfield Rifle & Carbine 1882
Rules & Management, Springfield Rifle & Carbine 1898
Catalog of Firearms. U. S. Cartridge Company.
Catalog of Fire-Arms for the Collector, Satterlee.
Catalog of Harrington & Richardson.
Catalog of the Bullard Repeating Arms Company.
Catalog of Whitney Armory.
Complete Guide to Handloading, Sharpe.
Ideal Hand-Book, Lyman Gunsight Company.
The Machine Gun—Volume 1. Chinn.

Schuyler, Hartley & Graham,

Nos. 17 and 19 MAIDEN LANE,

P. O. BOX 1700.

New York, Oct 24 1874

Sharps Rifle Co
~~Hartford~~ Bridgeport

D'Sirs Will you please inform us if you have any Lee guns. We should like a model. Have you put any 45s in the works if so when will they be ready

Ys truly
M Hartley

Lee rifles were made under contract by Sharps.